Disclaimer:

This book is not meant for everyone. It is specifically written for people with dreams, goals, and ambitions to make a difference in their own lives and in the lives of others. Small-minded people will not appreciate this book. For the people who are ready to continue, let the journey begin!

"Your time is limited, so don't waste it living someone else's life. Don't be trapped by dogma – which is living with the results of other people's thinking.
Don't let the noise of others' opinions drown out your own inner voice. And most important, have the courage to follow your heart and intuition. They somehow already know what you truly want to become.
Everything else is secondary."
-Steve Jobs
1955-2011

"Your salary is the bribe they give you to forget your dreams."
-Chrisjan Peters

Contents

My Story

My name is Ali. I was a below average student all throughout elementary school and high school. I was held back in the first grade due to bad behavior and attention problems. I could only listen for 10-20 seconds without zoning out and losing focus. I got in trouble almost every week, getting in fights and achieving poor grades.

Fast forward to the eighth grade. I had been suspended seven times for reasons I don't even want to mention. I was completely lost and did not know what I wanted to do. Almost everyone in my life was looking down on me at that point, except some close family and friends. I was the kid that teachers told other students to stay away from. I took all my frustration out by misbehaving, and I was deliberately ending up in trouble time and time again.

I was upset because it was hard for me to pay attention while everyone else around me understood everything the teachers were saying. I was always getting 40's and 50's on my tests while the kids next to me were getting 80's and better. I knew how much longer I studied than they did, too. I was looking at my letter grades and I remember asking myself "Am I really the dumbest person in this classroom?" I was told by teachers and principals that I was headed nowhere and my that future was not bright. At the time I was in the eighth grade and was very vulnerable to what people said to me. I let them put me down and I did nothing to lift myself up. My confidence was awful and my attitude was awful too. I barely ended up graduating the eighth grade. I was off to high school with no clue what I was doing or how to go about anything. Summer came around and I still could not control my anger problems. I ended up in trouble outside of school as well.

Freshmen year rolled around and I wanted to change, so I decided to start playing a lot of sports. I played soccer and basketball, and I ran track. I kept myself busy through the entire school year so I could stay out of trouble. I was still doing very poorly in school; it almost felt like the teachers I had were speaking another language. I was told "Ali, you really won't get anywhere in life with your academic skills." One of the teachers even told me that I was the kid all the teachers talked about in the lunchroom.

At 14 years old, when you hear things like that, it gets to you mentally. It wasn't like I blew all my homework away and didn't try. I gave school a lot of effort. I just did not learn and absorb information the way everyone else did. I never believed that school was not for me until later on in life. It took me a very long time to pick up the pieces. I was told by everyone that I would be nothing without a college degree. In high school the teachers and administrators made it seem like you either go off to college or end up a homeless person on the side of the street.

It seemed like there was no way around it for me. I was stuck in a system that drove me crazy. I eventually stopped getting in trouble due to all the extracurricular activities I signed up for. I spent every day either in the gym after school or on the field. Eventually I got pretty good at sports. I was never really amazing, but all the work I was putting in was starting to pay off. I was getting offers from colleges to run track and field my junior year, and then come my senior year they started flooding in.

I thought I had it made. I told myself that was my ticket and I was going to do whatever it took to run track in college, even if it meant dragging myself through four years of school. Track and field season came around and I was one of the top triple jumpers in the section for the state of New Jersey. I was getting a lot of attention at the time, and it was the best I ever felt in high school. I finally found something I wanted to do, and I enjoyed doing it.

The track and field season came closer to an end, which meant the state championship was getting closer. I was zoned in 100% on track and nothing else. At that point I settled with all C's when it came to my classes. I did that just so I could still participate in track and field. I was still lost, but I just did not know it. I wish I knew then the things that I now; but I didn't.

I spent 5-6 hours a day just training and getting ready for the state section championship. The first round were the relay championships for the long jump and triple jump events. We ended up winning both, coming in first place out of 50 schools. Then came the individual rounds, and that's when I really wanted to take first and become a champion. As corny as it sounds, that was the moment I had trained three years for.

I didn't play video games, have a girlfriend, or even attend a high school party. All I knew was sports. While I was in season, I was also in the recruiting process. I went down the list of colleges that wanted me to jump for them and started visiting them on the weekends to see where I wanted to go. After all the searching and matching, I sat down with my head coach along with my family and decided to commit to Utica University out in New York. I planned to go there for four years and run track and field while I dragged myself through four years of school. Utica had a great jumping program, and they had just opened the second biggest stadium for indoor track and field in North America. That was going to be my new home. After all this was set and stone, I got myself mentally ready for the next round of competition and headed back home.

So, the day finally came and I was ready to set a personal record! I was so pumped up that my adrenaline was through the roof! I never felt as good as I did that day when it came to being prepared. I knew I was going to kill all my competition when it came to the triple jump. There was a line of 112 kids jumping and we were lined up in pre-rank orders, meaning best jumper all the way down to the worst, determined by past jumps. I was the first one in line. As I looked back, I realized there was a reason I was

1st out of 112. I worked for that while people were out partying. I was grinding. Just looking back at the line gave me such a confidence boost because I knew I was going to set a new personal record before the jump. I ran down the runway faster than ever before. But after my first jump, I lost my footing and slipped going full speed. It felt like slow-motion until I landed. I landed on the side of my leg so hard it felt like my shin had exploded! I got helped off the runway, and it was at that point that I put my head in my hands and knew it was over. There was no way I would be able to compete for the rest of the season, which was only two more weeks.

Track and field was everything I knew. I didn't know what to do after I got hurt. After the ER, and finding out I fractured my shin, I was told by the doctor not to put any pressure on my leg. Things started to hit me, and I started to realize there was so much more to life than running down a track and jumping. I was good at it, but I knew it wasn't going to make me a living. My work ethic was great, but there was a peak to my skills on the track. And I had obtained them. I hit the ceiling. I realized I had an ego just from being the best in a tiny section of New Jersey. I had to really take a step back and evaluate my life. I was 18, had I terrible grades. I had no idea what I wanted to do with my life.

I was completely lost. But now that I look back at it, I am so happy I was lost. I will tell you exactly why further into this book. I started to ask myself, "Do I really want to go to a university just to compete in a sport?" If I were to get hurt like that in college, they would take all my scholarships away and tell me to have a nice day. They needed to use me for their school team, and that was it. I would be useless to them if I got hurt. I still hated school but I knew I had to go because at that moment I believed without a degree I would make no money and live a life of regret. That's what I was taught my whole life.

Man, was I wrong! That was one of the best things that could have happened to me, because if I'd never been hurt that day I would not be where I am today. I would have fed off the compliments, fed my ego, and attended the school. That wasn't my last endeavor when it came to falling and failing, but that was just one of many events that brought me to where I am now.

At the time, my mindset was that I wanted to make my parents happy and have a degree so I could live a comfortable life. I decided not to go to Utica University, and instead, I decided to attend a community college near where I lived. I barely graduated high school, and that summer I decided to really sit down and figure out what I loved to do. I knew I had learned so much from sports that I could not let all of it go to waste. I was a good leader and captain. A lot of people told me I motivated them and that was something that made me happy. So I sat there and did research on what kind of people help motivate other people and are, in a way, captains who have control over their decisions and work ethic. I wanted to transfer what I knew in sports to real life. When I did my research, I came across the word *entrepreneur*. I swear to you I'd never heard that word in high school in my life. When I saw the definition online and it said, "Someone who organizes and operates a business or businesses, taking on greater than normal financial risk in order to do so." I was ready to dive in head-first. I started watching videos on famous entrepreneurs all around the world, and I fell in love with their life-styles. I wanted to do everything they were doing.

So I decided, *That's it! I'm going to be an entrepreneur.* I'll shimmy my way through college just like I did in middle school and high school, and when I come out I'm going to have a wonderful business set up that's going to make me millions. Man, I was so wrong!

I ended up spending that summer researching and finding what I wanted to do. Finally, I knew I wanted to start my own brand for a product I really believed in. My close friend from high school, Murtaza and his older brother Mustafa, were doing very well in business, and I pitched a plan to them to start a business. They were in! We came together and researched what we wanted to do. One idea that came up was how men have started growing their beards out. It was a time everyone was growing a beard (or at least trying to). So we decided we were going to form a company selling beard products online, and we called the company mA Beard Co. We did a lot of research and optimized a brand that was unique to the beard-growing industry.

We came out with a beard oil called "growth formula." This formula had essential oils that helped hair growth and strengthen hair. I learned more from Murtaza and Mustafa in a few months than I did in all of middle school and high school. I finally started doing something I enjoyed and I had a passion for. It was an amazing experience. I met with a big time beard oil manufacturer in New York City. We did our research and found that he manufactured one of the best-selling formulas for beard oils. Then I set up a meeting to see him and talk about what our goals where and what we wanted to do.

When I arrived in New York City, I walked into his building, and that's one of the moments I will never forget in my life. The elevator opened to his office, which had a huge white floor with marble white walls, and he had an astonishing view of Times Square. I never thought I would be meeting with an owner of a big time manufacturing facility, in his office one-on-one, talking business. And I was just 18 years old! It was something that never crossed my mind because, in high school, the only thing that was on my mind was track and field and wasting my time at school. The second I stepped out of my comfort zone and decided to do something different, so many doors opened.

We came to an agreement, and Murtaza and I made our first order together. We ordered a variety of three products. One being a beard balm and the other two being beard oils. The process of bringing all the pieces together is what fascinated me. We bought bottles from China, labels from Florida, and the actual product from New York. That was something I had never done before, and when the final product was done it felt and looked amazing!

I felt like there was no ceiling to what we were doing. Everything was great until obstacles started to come along. I had never done business before, and from watching others, I thought everything was going to be a walk in the park. I thought we were going to start taking over the "e-commerce world." I was watching all these videos online and I was seeing all these Instagram posts of entrepreneurs living their lives to the fullest. But what I did not see was the work they put in behind the scenes. They worked day and night. They chose to struggle for 100 hours a week, starting with nothing and making nothing, instead of living a comfortable and promising lifestyle. They would stay up for 20 hours straight working hard, and then they would go to sleep only to wake up a few hours later to repeat the cycle all over again. They were grinding 24/7, and there was no one in the world who could stop them.

I was starting to lose it again and started to doubt myself because I did not have that type of work ethic. I started to put myself down instead of motivating myself. The work I was doing slowed down and within three months I fell off my workload. The business was going nowhere, and I let it get to me. If I could go back now, I would have done things differently. I would not have stopped because what we had built was awesome and it had massive potential. But I had a false vision of how business worked, and, truth be told, I had a lousy work ethic.

Business is kind of like a roller coaster. There are ups and downs. We had experienced a down phase and I didn't keep my composure. After that, my partners and I went our separate ways, but still very close friends to this day. The business was not working out so we dissolved our LLC. The business we had started ended up failing, and it was one that taught me many lessons now that I look back on. Murtaza and Mustafa continued to work hard despite the bumps in the road, and today Murtaza is the CEO of a company called Sparta Nutrition, which can be found at www.spartanutrition.com. They have one of the best supplement brands on the market and have products in every major supplement retail shop in the world!

Now, after the business failed, I was back in school and it was getting a little easier because I was spending a lot of time with tutors who helped me, multiple times a week. I still hated school with a passion, and I knew I did not need any of the things I was actually learning for real life situations. I felt like a robot every day. I was done with mA Beard Co. And now my mindset was back on that old routine—let me take the easy road. Let me get average grades and get done with college so I can get a job.

All I was thinking about was a job. I was starting to settle mentally, even before I hit 20 years old! School had beat me into a mindset that I was going to be an employee, not a boss. My major was Business Administration, and everyone who had that degree that I knew were making a salary of about $40-50k. I knew that, and I was still going to school. I was starting to get comfortable. I was starting to fall into the system of society, and I was headed down the road to becoming a robot just like the majority of people I knew. I continued to go to college, and I was now on my third year in a two-year school because of how poorly I did my first year.

I was finally almost done with community college, and I decided I was going to attend Rutgers University. That's what I set my mind on. I was ready to take out a $60,000 loan in order to obtain my bachelor's degree. I was still lost and just did not know it.

I was starting to get good at being a slave to the system. I was fitting in perfectly now. My creativity was going out the window, and I was just doing everything I was commanded to do. When I sat in my classes, I knew I had a special ability, something that was different from everyone else, but I was trying so hard to be like the people I was in class with. I was telling myself that those are the people who are going to be successful, that I needed to stop thinking differently, and that I should let my creative mindset go.

Now that I look back at it, I wish I could go back and smack my old self on the back of the head. However, I stayed that way. Graduation came around and I was ready to go to Rutgers University. I had gotten accepted on instant decision day, and at the time I believed that was the right move for me.

I prepared to graduate from community college, and the day before graduation my phone rang. It was a call from my school administrator, and he told me I had to come in for a meeting with him at 6:00 pm that Thursday night, which was a day before graduation. He wouldn't tell me the reason over the phone, but he wanted me to come in and speak to him privately. So, I went in and he had a stack of papers in his hands. He sat me down and told me the scholarships I had been receiving for the last two years have been voided because they were not filled out properly when I signed up for them two years ago. He claimed I owed everything I received in the last two years in about a month and a half after graduation. He also said I wouldn't get my diploma until I paid off the debt.

It was at that moment that it all hit me like never before. Everything that I went through with school... And then they come up with this. I could understand if they told a student a month after the problem happened, but to wait two years and then a day before graduation to unleash everything on them is just cruel. I saw the date the problem was revealed, and it was not anywhere near when I was graduating. I was shocked. But at the same time, I couldn't believe they pulled a fast one on me like that. It wasn't just me, there was a whole line of students outside the office waiting to be called in.

I decided to go home. I sat down and thought to myself, *School really is a business and certain kids are getting scammed.* I then asked myself, *What can I do to make a difference and help people open their eyes, and show this to the world?* That's when I told myself that I was going to do everything I could to never have to go back to school. I was going to help people realize how much of a scam college in America really is. I never knew the U.S. was $1.5 trillion in debt as of 2018 when it came to student loan debt. There are college alumni suffering with student loan debt and hate their job at the age of 40. That was where I was headed if God didn't help me see things in new ways.

So I decided to take a stand and show the world what I thought about college and the school system. I made a video of myself talking about why I believe college is a scam, especially for business students. Oh, and then to spice things up I paid my debt in 25,000 quarters and put the video on YouTube. That's when I knew there was no going back. I took the initiative. Every day when I woke up from that point on I was ready to do whatever it took to never have to even think about going back.

In the future I would love to create a school that's actually made to help a student grow and evolve in the unique way they were built. I would like to create a school where students get to choose what they like to do and really concentrate on that. I hate to see talented kids get stuck and cornered in something they are terrible at. If you have 23 kids in a classroom, it's obvious that all 23 have their own unique abilities. To have them all focus on one topic makes no sense to me. The world would be such a different place if everyone did what they were good at and only worked at making themselves amazing at it.

The longer you stay in that system the harder it becomes to step out of your comfort zone. Why does one have to take classes that have nothing to do with what they are trying to become? After I was done saying what I had to say and paying my debt off in quarters, I told myself I would never go back. Every day since the incident, I've woken up and, attacked my day like I had a chip on my shoulder. I have this burst of energy every morning, and I always will because I started to finally believe in myself! I didn't think about what anyone had to say about me. I started to finally step outside my comfort zone. I started reading and doing things I thought I never would. I read almost 2-3 books every month on average since dropping out. I also started my own e-commerce business and started making decent money from it.

I then invested in a class in New York City called StockMarketLab, and it was one of the best investments I have ever made! The class was hands on and was interesting from the start to the end. One class was from 8:00 am to 3:00 pm, and I was zoned in the whole time because I knew I could apply what I learned there to real life and make money from it. If I hadn't taken that class I probably would never have written this book. The class had nothing to do with writing, but the founder, Umar Ashraf, ended up becoming more than just a swing/day trading teacher. He became my mentor. He helped me build confidence, and he really showed me that anything is possible if the work ethic is there. He helped me learn stocks, which I've benefited from tremendously. Learning this trait is something that will serve me for the rest of my life as a separate source of income. For what I remember, school did not teach me a single thing about money and money management, let alone how taxes work or how to manage your time.

This was something that I would never have thought about doing if I was still in school. I would go to school and then go straight home like a zombie. I would have done the same routine every day and that would be it. I felt like a zombie, and I saw it every day, not just in myself but the other students around me. The majority of students I knew were not where they wanted to be in life, and they were not working to get to where they wanted to be. I am finally doing everything I want to do at the age of 22, and I am only just starting! I finally grew the confidence to get out of my comfort zone and take risks that I would never see myself taking before.

I started a CBD company called Allevi8te with my brother. We started having sit down meetings every week, and before we knew it we were working 15+ hours a day and really started to click. The company is centered on CBD products, which is short for cannabidiol. Cannabidiol is all natural and has medical and therapeutic benefits as well. Cannabidiol can help ailments such as inflammation, migraines, anxiety, joint pain, and seizures, as well as many others. If interested, the products can be found on www.allevi8te.com. Cannabidiol has helped ease many people with breast cancer, lung cancer, and many more illnesses. Cannabidiol is now federally legal in all 50 states, and it's only starting to find its place in the market. We only offer broad spectrum products which means they contain no THC. It is a very safe substance to use. My favorite part about it is that it has benefits that help fight against cancer. I will talk more about it in detail further into the book.

I've had many ups and downs in life not knowing where to go and what to do. The reason I am writing this book is to help the youth and even the elderly understand their value in achieving the goals and dreams that are within their grasp and how they can obtain them. The school system and the way society is built is a barrier to freedom. Financial freedom is a big aspect of life, but if you're stuck behind a desk making just enough to scrape by and you're consuming all your energy and time doing it, then where do you think that's going to lead you?

Everyone on this planet has a dream and everyone has a vision, but only a small percentage go out and chase it. I do not think life is going to get any easier or that I have accomplished anything because this is only the start. But I know I have the mindset to think differently and chase anything I want if I put my mind to it. In this book I am going to tell you why that is, and how you can too chase your dreams and ambitions if you follow some very simple rules and guidelines.

One of my biggest visions in my life is to help others to the best of my ability, whether it's through professional or financial influence. Not everyone on the planet is as blessed as you and me are. We are blessed to have water and food every day. Not everyone has that. Wouldn't you want to help individuals who are suffering? Set yourself up so you can set others up because there is no better feeling in the world than helping others and seeing them change for the better due to the help you provided them.

Chapter 1: Why Many Students Do Not Succeed In the School System

If you take a look around the room you're in right now, and just imagine what it looked like 50 years ago, you would see a world of a difference. Try it. Just close your eyes for a few seconds and imagine the year is 1970. Your iPhone would not be there; your laptop would not exist. Your lighting would be different. Everything would be different because the world has changed immensely since that time. Everything is evolving and changing rapidly. Now, if you look at a picture of a classroom from 1969 and then compare it to today's classroom, you will see no difference except the way people dress. You would see a teacher by a board and a bunch of kids raising their hands in their seats. Why has the school system never really changed? Why do kids still have problems trying to figure out what the teacher is teaching? Why do some students hate school? Why are kids forced to learn one way?

These are questions that should be raised and dealt with. Do you have to do certain things in life that you will hate? Yes, but the fact that school is what raises most people and molds them into the adults they become makes it all the more important. School should really be evaluated at all levels and should be constantly evolving and changing. I'm not trying to say school is the root of all evil and that no one should go to school. But I'm saying there needs to be a turnaround in the way it's constructed both for students and teachers. Students should be able to choose what they like to do and focus on things they're good at, instead of living their lives focusing on their weaknesses from a young age.

If LeBron James played four sports instead of focusing on basketball, he would not have the dominant carrier that he has. The reason is because he would have diversified his time and effort playing and practicing other sports than basketball, and that would have taken away from him getting better at basketball. He might have played multiple sports when he was young, but when he got to 14-15 years old and knew basketball was his passion, he focused on that. The same should apply with school. If a student finds that he is fascinated with robotics and he knows that's what he wants to do, why is he only allowed to take one class out of eight a day on robotics?

If students could focus on their strengths and really learn the ins and outs of the field they are in or want to be in, then the world would be a different place. Students would enjoy going to school. They would be learning what they like instead of being forced to learn things that won't even suit them further down the road. Each student in a classroom has their own unique ability. It's currently the 21st century, and everything is evolving so rapidly. There are 10-year-olds making 6-7 figures on YouTube producing videos for their channels! I promise you that school did not teach them how to do that. Why should one not be taught how to start their own YouTube channel and vlog? If that's something a student wants to do, they should be taught everything from how production works down to editing and everything else that comes along with it. If a student wants to do that, they need to learn how to act, use a camera, edit, and have very creative ideas to produce to the world for the taking. They should still have to take core classes for understanding and growth, but to sit in a social studies class and listen to an old man reminisce and cheer about how he felt when he was in Vietnam is a total waste for most students. If there are 30 students in the class and only two like and enjoy what the old man is talking about, the other 28 are taking time away from their strengths and losing valuable time by "listening" to what the old man has to say. Instead they could be working on what they are good at and become great at it!

When I was in school, I personally enjoyed the concept of how marketing worked. I wanted to learn everything about marketing down to the bone. So I decided to sign up for a marketing class, which cost me $1,700 at a community college (which is rated as one of the top colleges in my state). What did that marketing class consist of and how long was the marketing class? First of all, the marketing class that I took in college consisted of learning about making ads that go in the newspaper and how marketing worked previously. The class was only six weeks long. Then, at the end of the semester, I had to present what my ad was and how I would put it in the paper myself. Oh, and also, the professor teaching marketing class was definitely 70+ years old. How does this make any sense? We live in a time where most people can't look at a newspaper without throwing up. Why would I advertise my business on something that only a very small portion of humanity looks at? Wouldn't I want to advertise my business on Facebook or Instagram, where there are more than one billion active users? I honestly don't think the professor even knew what social media was or how many people promoted their businesses on it, let alone understood how it worked. My mindset mid-way through the class at the time was, what an easy way to get three credits. Let me get a good letter grade and move on. That was the mindset of the five people sitting around me as well. We were just in the class to get by, get a letter grade, and move onto the next class just so we could take one class, to get one credit closer to getting that piece of paper they call a bachelor's degree. I was learning useless information and paying for it. Worst of all, I was wasting precious time!

Things have changed since the 1990's. Things have changed since 2018, and it's currently 2019. When you read this it may be well past 2019, but you get the point. Brick and mortar stores are shutting down. Big time retail stores are going out of business, and everyone is shopping online. Does what I just mentioned raise some questions in your head? Students are learning useless information and they are paying top dollar for it. I have friends who have taken loans out for a $100,000 for a bachelor's degree in business administration. Today they get paid $40,000 a year before taxes. How does that make any sense? They made a $100,000 investment, spend 4-5 years in school, and they get a return of $40,000 a year. They have to be a slave to some boss in a suite that may not be a nice person. Maybe there are only a few people who see it like I do.

I understand it's scary to take risks. But without risks your comfort zone will always be your best friend. You will always be looking to be safe and comfortable. When in reality, safety is nothing but an illusion. You can work for the best company and have a spectacular degree. If the economy was to crash, I promise you the beautiful company you work for would not think twice before letting you go unless you brought something to the table no one else could. But college doesn't raise you that way. You are bringing what hundreds of thousands of other college graduates are bringing to the table. I'm sorry, but the truth is ugly sometimes. In college you are sitting and learning what the person next to you is. What makes you any different? You better be doing something outside the classroom that will set you apart.

The student sitting next to you can do the same thing you can. Now multiply that by the students around the world taking the same class as you and learning the same things as you while trying to obtain the same degree you are. You may get luckier than the person sitting next to you and land a better job and have a better career and "benefits." But do you really want to hope to get lucky or do you want to go after what can be yours?

There are certain degrees that require going through school, such as becoming a doctor or lawyer. But to go to school as an undecided major and waste both your time and money is foolish. Students are learning things they won't even apply to their day-to-day lives. I hate to see so many students waste their time every day, clueless and not knowing what they are doing or want to do, hoping they get lucky. It's a system that's set up for a majority of people to not do well in. At the same time, it's a system almost everyone goes through. There is no denying going to school when you are a kid. But as you get older, you have a choice. Most students think they don't have a choice because of what their parents say or what they think their future might be like without that piece of paper. They may be too scared to take the jump. Whatever the case may be, if school is not doing you justice and it's just holding you back from chasing and achieving your goals and ambitions in life, why keep wasting your time?

How to Overcome the School System and Head in a Successful Direction

(1) Technology is soaring like never before.

There has never been a time in the past when technology has been as powerful as it's today. And only God knows how much more advanced it's going to get in the near future. That being said, spend your time researching what you like instead of watching Netflix and scrolling through Instagram! Pick up that laptop or smart phone and start researching things that fascinate you. You should not have to have a professor pushing you or holding your hand. If that's the case, school is perfect for you. Start learning about things that you actually like on your own time. Stop procrastinating and just start doing it. It doesn't start tomorrow or next week. It starts now. If you are reading this and are thinking about actually doing the research, let me just tell you, you are late. You should have started a long time ago. So now that you are behind, spend double the time you normally would and start now.

You will always be behind when first starting something. It is your job to catch up and get ahead. Do not let being behind discourage you, but let it help you build a drive to get ahead. You can find all the information you want online. You can find endless information and it's mostly all free! It's on the table for the taking, but we live in a time where everyone is absorbed in technology the wrong way. Students and civilians are spending hours on end watching Netflix and are so into watching other people lives on social media that it's taking away from their own lives. It's stopping them from getting to where they need to be. It boggles my mind to see all of this. Use technology to your advantage instead of letting it be used against you. You will see how far that will take you just by itself.

(2) Find a mentor

Just like I said at the beginning of the book, I met a mentor, Umar, and it was not like I was looking. I was just trying to take a class outside of school on stocks, but I got so much more from it. Will you randomly bump into someone like that? Maybe not. But if you go out of your comfort zone, you may just happen to meet someone that can help you towards a successful path. You don't even have to meet someone in person; you can meet a mentor online today! YouTube has millions of videos of successful entrepreneurs, leaders, coaches, etc., explaining how they got to where they are at in life. They can help you obtain what they have. I was told that reading was one of the most important aspects when it comes to becoming successful. I never thought reading was important. I never read a single book throughout elementary, middle, and high school because I was assigned it. Every summer when I was assigned summer reading, I would either not do it or

I would pay someone to do it for me. Now I have read 100+ books on business, life, and so on.

I always thought reading was lame and for nerds. When I was introduced to reading from a different viewpoint, I started to take notice of the impact it can have. In school the thinking was, you better read or you will get detention. After high school I started watching a lot of videos on YouTube about successful people. I watched all these successful entrepreneurs like Bill Gates, Elon Musk, etc., and, learned about how they obtained their success. They would talk about how many books they've read, how far it's taken them in life, and what type of growth they've encountered from reading.

It completely changed my point of view. I started reading, and instantly I felt my mind growing. I felt a lot more knowledgeable on the topics I was reading about. I started to communicate better vocally after spending so many years being shy and quiet. Reading has helped me tremendously in life; even the way I carry myself has changed. Reading has actually built my confidence, and it has helped me get out of my comfort zone. I would not be writing this book or running my businesses if I had never started reading. When I started my first business, I had no knowledge. I just dove into it. It was a great experience, but it was going to fail long before it even launched. I did not know what I was in for and had no idea what to do when things started to get rough.

(3) Find an idea that really interests you and draws you in

Everyone is different in their own way. So, don't follow someone just to follow them. Make sure the mentor you choose is someone you see yourself being like or someone who will help you obtain the vision you have. Grasp the ideas you have. Now it's time to chase them. You won't ever have today back, let alone the years that have already flown by. You only have so much time on earth. Not knowing when you will depart only gives you so much time to make things happen.

So start today! If you do not want to be a part of a system where you spend your life working for others, then you better be ready to bring something to the table that will impact the world. You can't have zero credentials, procrastinate, and have no clue on what you want to do. That is what will make you lose your mind. You have to see progress in order to mentally believe in yourself and strive to accomplish the things you are trying to accomplish. So, that means you have to be different.

Not many people read. According to inc.com, the average person reads a book a year, and a CEO reads a book a week! The fact that you have taken the time out of your day to open this book and read it makes you one in a million already. There is so much opportunity today with the way the world is evolving; it's incredible. Learn what you want, do what you want, and live the way you want! In order to do that you need to find what interests you and what you see yourself doing for the rest of your life.

(4) Work like you've never worked before.

If you're looking to run your own business and be your own boss, there's no guaranteed $50,000+ a year waiting for you anymore. It's either you go get what's yours or there is nothing waiting for you on the other side. That's why many people are not willing to get out of their comfort zone and really chase their ambitions. There's no guidance counselor holding your hand and telling you, "Hey, you need to obtain a certain letter grade so it looks like your resume is worth reading." You're on your own, with no help.

You should sit there and ask yourself before you decide to skip out on school or the corporate life, if you are ready for the hustle, both mentally and physically. I promise you will destroy yourself if you are not mentally ready, let alone physically ready. You need to be ready for early mornings and late nights. You need to be ready to say no to your friends when they want to watch the football games all Sunday. You need to be ready to say no to the parties you are invited to.

The people indulging in these activities are most likely going to find a job. You are trying to create work. So, your mind has to be on another level when it comes to making the decisions you make. If your thought is, "I'm not going to go to college, but something will come my way, hopefully," you're in for a long ride. If you are someone saying, "I will eventually leave my job one day when things are good," then you will probably end up back in college and on your way to being a slave to the system within a few months. If you are waiting for the perfect time to leave your job, it's never going to come. Things don't just happen in life. You need to be willing to take risk. Nothing pisses me off more than when people say, "Hopefully I make it." Not that having hope is bad or anything, but people say it like a wish and they are hoping things just fall into their lap. You have to go out and get what's yours or someone else will just do it. It's that simple.

(5) Don't let others put you down.

There are going to be people who put you down no matter what you do in life. When it comes to making big decisions in life, do what your gut is telling you, not what the person sitting next to you is saying. Unfortunately, we live in a world where people do not want the best for you, or if they do, they want you to do what they want. That being said, a lot of the time it's the people surrounding you. People will always try to tell you not to chase your dreams and go after what you want to do in life. Rather, they will tell you to take the safe route. Maybe your parents will, maybe your siblings or close friends will say these things. However, it's up to you to make the change and chase whatever it is you are trying to do. I personally believe safety is an illusion. There is no such thing as real safety. Anything can happen at any moment. How do you know the economy won't crash? How do you know a huge war won't break out? How do you know the company you work for won't shut down? To me there is no safe route, so I encourage people to take risk because with big risk comes big rewards.

There is no telling what will happen even within the next few seconds. So, how is one going to tell you to take the safe route so you can have a secure future? There is a reason the most successful people in the world are where they are. They took massive risks along with massive action; they stayed quiet and worked hard. Talk is cheap; they actually went out and did it. They believed in their dreams and they did whatever it took to achieve them. Those people are the 1% of the population. The rest of humanity is too caught up on what their neighbor, Billy, may think of them or what could possibly go wrong if they took the risk.

If you live your life thinking about the negative things that could happen, I promise you, life will only hand you more problems. If you have a positive mindset and are always working on growing and improving, you will only find yourself in a better world. Be happy for others when they achieve success! Be the one to help them achieve that success, whatever it may be in whichever way you possibly can. Energy always comes around. If you are positive, you will see positive results. But if you are negative, you will only see negative results. That being said, don't let anyone tell you what you can and can't do.

(6) Confidence is key!

All throughout my days growing up, my confidence was repeatedly destroyed by teachers and principals. I was put down and did nothing about it. I never lifted myself up either until later on in life. I would get back my test grades and my results would affect my confidence. I was letting my confidence be destroyed left and right due to a letter grade that, at the time, defined success.

One of the reasons confidence is very important is because confidence is what will help you feed your ambition and fuel your drive. A letter grade should never determine your future. Not everyone is a good test taker. I know I wasn't. But what I did know was that I was good at other things. However, I would get back my test and when I would look at the results everything would change. I would start to think negatively about myself and it only got worse as I got older. Going through school really did not give me any confidence to achieve any sort of success. I had to figure out how I was going to build confidence on my own and how I was going to have the drive to achieve the things I wanted in life.

The school system is not for everyone. People learn in their own ways. To be forced to learn one way is brutal. Now let me ask you a question, Can a fish climb a tree? Of course not. My three-year-old nephew can tell me the answer to that question. When I was in school I felt like a fish trying to climb a tree, in a way. I could not do what I was told to do, and I was not built to grasp what I was being taught. School was not for me. I have realized there are many students who are like the fish, but they continuously try to climb the tree instead of realizing they are good at swimming. They spend their whole lives trying to climb that tree without realizing how far they could have gone in life if they just worked on becoming great swimmers.

Stop what you are doing and just ask yourself if you love what you do. Whether you are a student or a have a job. Really ask if you see yourself doing what you are doing for the rest of your life. Because if you cannot see yourself doing it, then you will run into big problems in the future. You will live a very stressful life working for money, most likely living paycheck to paycheck. I hear a lot students say, "I can't wait to make $60,000 a year!" They are willing to do anything to obtain that yearly income, which, in reality is not a lot considering the time we live in. They are willing to trade time for money. That is how you set yourself up to work for money and not have money work for you. You will spend your entire day in a cubical helping someone else become rich. Is that what you want?

One of my favorite quotes is by Tony Gaskins: "If you don't build your dream someone will hire you to help build theirs." Think about that for a second. I don't care how old you are. You still are breathing and you have the chance to do whatever it is that will help you achieve your ambitions. It may not have anything to do with making a lot of money, but if you have been thinking about doing something and have not done it yet, then you are letting something hold you back. You may never get a chance, because you spent your whole life waiting for the perfect moment. There will never be a perfect time. There's never a perfect time to start a business. There is never a perfect time to get married. There is never a perfect time to have a kid. Life will never hand you a perfect moment. You just have to go out and do it. Take the risk and without a doubt you will see results. They may not be positive right away, but even the negative results will help you obtain positive ones if you take your losses and turn them into lessons.

School has structured people to live by a system. In school you are told what to do every day. You are told when to learn, eat, and run. The school system is so structured in a way it seems like a prison. There are bells after every class and public security walking the halls all day. When students see freedom they are not prepared for it. School does not prepare you to survive on your own. Instead, school is a process of learning, memorizing, and utilizing, whereas the real world is all about doing and taking action.

You can be a straight A student and still not know how to survive on your own and work efficiently. The reason is because the straight A student spent his or her life being perfect when it came to school and getting grades.

However, they may not have something called "street smarts" or "common sense." People who are street smart know their way around. They can identify other people's behaviors. They can tell what is going on in their surroundings and they are always ready for something to happen. They know what to do in a situation before the situation even occurs.

The "book smart" person is good at what he or she knows but is clueless when it comes to basic things in the real world. Really take a moment to read this quote and think about the successful people you may know or heard of. "The A students work for the B's, the C's run the companies, and the D students dedicate the buildings." This is from Paul Orfalea. What does that tell you? Being an A student will not make you super successful, and that was a huge misconception I had my whole life. I thought all the students in my classes doing so much better than I was were going to have a bright future and I was going to be left behind.

I was brainwashed to believe my grade point average was everything and how it would make or break me as a person in society. That is what most students are taught in the school system. Most C students are willing to taking a risk and fail. While A students have never fallen and they want to do everything the perfect way. A students like to follow directions and the guidelines that are given to them. C students will create and take a risk in whatever it is they are trying to do. C students are automatically out of their comfort zone while A students feel very accomplished and happy with what they have achieved. Letter grades should not determine a student's success because once a student is entitled to something, especially at a young age, it's very hard for them to change their ways as they get older. If you are told you are a failure your whole life, you will most likely tell yourself you are a failure down the road. Only very few will recognize they have something special. If teachers tell students they are failures, then that's exactly how they will start thinking of themselves.

The system really needs to be evaluated and changed. The world is growing and moving so fast while we still have the same school systems. It's up to us if we want to make that change. The system will never change until people start raising their voices. The problem is not just the school system; it's the fact that majority of people are getting super comfortable with life. They admire the system because it sets them up to have a "safe job" when in reality it just turns humans into robots in most cases. People are setting themselves up to help others get rich, while they are stuck doing the same thing they hate every day. They are stuck limiting their lives and wasting time they will never get back.

Chapter 2: Live Your Life How You See It

Do not spend your life trying to please everyone and make them happy. Many college students, when asked why they go to school, will say things like; "My parents made me" or "I don't want to make my parents upset, so I'm here." Their mindset is, they are going to graduate to make their parents happy and then they are going to venture off and do their own thing after graduation. It does not work like that. At the age of 18-22, you are at a vital time in your life, and you can do a lot if you put your mind to it. Between the ages of 18-22 most people do not have kids or a mortgage to pay for. When you are 19 you can make more mistakes and still keep going.

As you get older you have more responsibilities and overhead that will be holding you back from taking leaps, such as starting your own business and taking on the venture you always had in mind. Find what it is that you like to do and go out and do it. Tell your parents or close ones, "This is what I want to do." At the end of the day, it's your life. No one should tell you how to live your life. If you are straight-forward with your parents or whomever it may be, and you have a business plan or idea on what you want to do, there is no reason they should stop you. The reason my parents did not mind that I dropped out was because they knew I had a crazy work ethic. Where they happy? No, they wanted me to graduate and get a degree so I could get a suitable job.

The reason they stopped getting mad was that they saw me waking up on a schedule and working when no one told me to. They witnessed me working late nights and early mornings. I dropped out, but on average I would still spend 20+ hours a week in the library. I decided it was that time in my life to start working hard. I took the initiative, and I wish I had done it earlier because only God knows where I'd be today otherwise. You can't live your entire life making others happy. If you are living your life always trying to make others happy, you will never truly get to do what you want to do in life. There are certain decisions in life you have to make on your own for your own sake.

Make decisions on your own, even if they may not be the best ones. The reason I am saying this is that you will learn from the mistakes and decisions you make. If the decisions are made for you already, then there is no learning curve. If there is no learning curve, then you can't lose and there can be no growth. I see students all the time that cannot make a single decision in life for themselves. They have everything planned out for them and they just follow what's been planned for them. When you were young you were told to be a leader, not a follower, right? Everyone has heard that before. Then why are most people being followers and doing what everyone else is doing? Be a leader, set a tone, and tell yourself you can do it, even if no one else believes in you. Do not live your life in other people's image. Your parents or close ones may be upset if you tell them college or the job you have is not for you, but when they see that you are making a difference and working hard, they will be happy. Am I saying not to go to college and do nothing? NO! Go to school if you do not know how to take care of yourself day-to-day. Do not skip out on school or a 9-5 job if you are going to spend your time sleeping and procrastinating.

You have one life to live on this planet and that's it. You will never get today back. Let that sink in for a moment. If you are spending all your time trying to make everyone happy, you will not be able to live life how you see it. You will be stuck trying to please everyone and the only person that will not be pleased is you. I am not saying to be a cruel or selfish person, but set yourself up when you are young so that when you are older you can do the things you always wanted to do, whatever that may be. Go out and do whatever it takes to live the life you want. If you see yourself starting an online business, go and do it! Stop telling yourself that you will do it in the future when things are better. Things never get better until you decide to make them better. You have to make the jump and take the risk. There are way too many people in their 40's that are lost. What have they been doing their whole lives? They pissed away every chance they had at life, they spent their weekends going out, living paycheck to paycheck, and now they are running into a dead end. Life only hands you opportunities when you go out and seek them. Things do not just happen by themselves.

If you have a vision, go out and chase it. Stop wasting time just thinking about it. Many people have an idea/invention they think about. But only a few go out and actually try making it happen. That is what separates the successful people in the world from the average people. The average person has excuses; the successful person is visionary and believes in whatever it is he or she is working on. I have faith in every person who reads this book, but if you do not have faith in yourself, then you are and always will be doomed. I can believe in you as much as I want, but the second you start to doubt yourself you will not do what it takes and you will not take the jump that's needed. The reason I know that is because that was me a few years ago. I doubted myself and I was living for others. I listened to everything everyone told me. It was hard for me to make decisions on my own, do not let yourself be in this situation.

Learn to Say No

I lived a life that others saw me living, and not a life I saw myself living. I never knew how to say no. I always agreed to what everyone had to say. In order to grow and really go after whatever It is you are trying to do, then you cannot let people hold you back. When someone asks you if you want to go out on Friday night or whatever the case may be, and you know you have a lot of work to do, you need to be strong enough to say no. As corny as it sounds it's not easy, especially when you are young. You will start telling yourself you don't want to miss out on anything. You see everyone having fun on social media and talking about how crazy their weekend was. Its only human for you to want to join. If you do decide to skip out and work instead of going out, you now just took a major step toward growth. You took a huge step in having self-discipline. You had the courage to say no and instead you stayed home or at the office and worked on yourself and the venture you are trying to start. All that hard work will have positive results down the line. The fact that you said no will come back positively now because, instead of wasting a whole night like the majority of the people in the world are, you spent that time working.

Now I feel great when I miss out on what everyone else is doing because that's what the majority of the average people out there are doing. If you want to be great, why are you doing average things? Trying to be great and then doing all the average things everyone else is doing will only lead you to live like everyone else. I skipped the Super Bowl for years to work on what I had to do. Watching grown men wearing tights and playing football was not going to help me get closer to where I wanted to be. They were making a living and doing what they loved. But I wasn't. There were many big boxing marches and UFC fights I decided not to watch. I've never felt better because the time I would have wasted watching them I spent working on myself and my business. It made me feel good because I realized the whole world was so focused in on these events, and there only had to be a small percentage that were doing something different. The people you are watching on live TV worked their asses off. They didn't take a second to slow down, and that's why they are where they are in life. They deserve the million dollar contracts because they did something different. They hustled until it was time for them to be in the spotlight while everyone else was just fitting in and getting by.

The world seems so fascinated by these people they see on TV. Especially in America, everyone loves to see these celebrities like they have some type of "connection" with them. These celebrities don't know you even exist and if they saw you they would forget who you were 20 seconds later. It drives me crazy when I see people devote their lives to fantasy leagues and watching football all Sunday, every Sunday. Think about it, grown men wearing another man's name on their back and watching football like they were getting paid top dollar for it. There's nothing wrong with taking time off and relaxing. Football can be a hobby, but when you are in debt, over-weight, and working your way to your second divorce, the last thing you should be doing is watching another grown man make money while playing a sport. First, set yourself up and then take time to relax and enjoy life.

Do Not Be a Victim of the System

Have you ever had a real conversation with someone who works in the corporate world 9 to 5, Monday through Friday? If you haven't, ask them what their work life is like? They will either tell you they do nothing but watch YouTube all day after a few hours of working or they will tell you they feel abused with the work load their boss puts on them. Either one of those situations will tell you they are sucked out of doing something valuable for themselves. They will always be helping others become rich. It's like they are stuck in a maze and will never find their way out until they're 70. The reward at the end of the maze waiting for them is their 401k, which won't do them much good. They are a victim of the system and they may not even know it. I have many family members and close family friends who are a part of the system and do not know it. They think that's how life is supposed to be. You go to school, get a degree (show off the degree), get a job, get married, have kids, pay off your debts, and die. That's all life consists of in their books. They don't think about growing, expanding, changing, or traveling—none of that. They think about the same thing every day and go through the same routine with the same negative attitude.

We need to start taking a step back and evaluating life and what we can do in life to really change ourselves and make the world a better place. As Americans, we love to consume everything from food to materialistic belongings. The first step to getting out of the system is to get yourself out of debt. Stop buying junk you don't need. It's that plain and simple. Discipline yourself, and do not shop for things that are not necessities. Sure, it may look cool to wear a $500 belt, but what good does that do for you? That is $500 you can invest and do so much more with. Start thinking about things to do outside of the job you're stuck in or the school you are going to. Start thinking of ideas and a game plan for what your next move is going to be. If you do quit your job and tell your boss to F' off, and yet don't have an idea of what you want to do or a game plan, then you will be begging him to give you your job back a few months down the road. Save up while you work the job you hate. Suck it up. Don't waste your money on anything. When you feel like you have enough for the idea or venture you are looking into, then quit and don't look back. The most successful people in the world will tell you they are in the situation they are in because they took a jump.

Why work at a job that's just going to destroy your personal life and family life? Why work a 9 to 5 job, come home pissed off, watch TV, go to sleep, and then wake up to repeat the same thing over again? Why not work for yourself and be your own boss? Just tell yourself you can do it and really start to change your mindset. What makes you different from any of the most successful people on the planet? They have 24 hours in a day just like you and me. They have problems just like you and me. But they are amazing at whatever it is that they do. They have almost perfected their skills because they worked at them for so long and put everything into their own development. LeBron James was not an overnight success. He worked his whole life to get to where he is. He was raised in some of the poorest and most dangerous places in America. He still found a way to make it because he believed in himself way before he even made the NBA. He had a tattoo that said "the chosen one" on his back at 15 years old. He told himself he was going to make it and he believed it. His mindset was always positive, even when he was in the worst of situations.

You have to believe in yourself. Nothing kills dreams like doubt. Doubt will destroy your dreams more than failures will. I doubted myself when I started my first company and that's what drove it into the ground. The day I started to believe in myself and built confidence was the day my life turned around. I stopped listening to the critics; you need to know they will talk no matter what. You can become as successful as you want, but people will still talk bad about you. That is something you have to know, and you have to be able to block it out. Believe that you have the strength to leave the job or classes you are taking if they are not making you happy. Find something that you love to do and can see yourself doing for a long time and go for it. Have passion in whatever you are trying to do and do not let anyone tell you otherwise. One of the reasons the corporate world sucks the life out of workers is that most individuals are working just for a paycheck.

When you just work for money, you become a very depressed individual. You have no pleasure in the work you do. You think you will find yourself in a better place if you make more money. In reality, you will only find yourself more depressed. Money is great and a huge essential to life, but you have to love what you do.

Vision

Everyone on earth has visions and dreams but only a few try to obtain them. Everyone sees a happy version of themselves but continue to live a life they hate or know they will hate further down the road. It's your life. Find a way to make a change so you can chase your dreams and create the vision you have been seeing all along. Will you be lonely and depressed at times? Yes. But if you are working for a better life, it will be well worth it. If you are looking to make changes that will bring gratification and stabilization into your life, it will be well worth it. You will sacrifice a little for a lot, and that will set you up for life. Why live a lifestyle that will bring you crashing down in the future, indulging in spending rather than investing?

People who have a lot of liabilities and no assets are setting themselves up for failure. They know what they own has no return, but they continue to indulge in buying more useless stuff. Why not invest, especially when you are young? Investing smart will help you live an abundant lifestyle when you are older. I'm not saying you have to invest everything you have to your name, but at least invest so you can learn how it works. A lot of people have the mindset that they are going to invest when they make a lot of money. In reality, they will only spend more because they have never invested before and all they know how to do is spend. If you want to invest in stocks, research how stocks work and put in a few bucks and see how things play out. If you wait until you have a lot of money, you could be giving up potential time where you could have learned how the stock market works and how certain things work.

You can learn from your losses and grow if you get into investing when you are young. If you look at losses as lessons, then you can change your whole perspective on growing and striving for a better life. Every time you look at a loss as a failure and give up, you are only hurting yourself. But if you take a step back and evaluate your loss and see what you could have done better, the next time around you may not make the same mistake. If you give up, then you will never know where you could have ended up if you kept pushing and trying. You will not become an overnight success. You will see many failures before you see success, but when you finally see success you will realize why you needed the failures to be where you are. I see way too many people give up after their first attempt. They get upset and think it's not for them.

If your mindset is, "It had better work the first time I try," then you are in the wrong place. Especially when it comes to being an entrepreneur. It's awesome to tell people you are an entrepreneur or trying to become one. What many people do not know is being an entrepreneur comes with a lot of baggage. People do not realize or witness the sleepless nights and the financial difficulties one will encounter when becoming an entrepreneur. All your chips are in one basket, and you are trying to fight the odds against you. There is a lot of stress involved and sacrifices. People only see the posts on social media of these entrepreneurs traveling, but they see none of the backend work that's involved.

Sit back and really think about what it is you want to do and what you want to become. Now ask yourself if you are headed in the right direction to get there. Do not lie to yourself and say, "I am," but your major is in liberal arts and you are trying to become a businessman or you are working behind a desk full time and you want to become your own boss. Work on getting to wherever it is you see yourself. Do not lie to yourself. It will only destroy you. Be truthful to yourself, even when it hurts. Start to become ambitious.

Action

If you have a vision, it's now time you go out and chase it. Do not get lazy or side-tracked. Go after that vision and do not let a single person stop you. I had a vision that I wanted to write this book at 22. Is it perfect? Of course not. Will there be people who talk it down and laugh about it? Of course there will be. But I had a vision that I was going to write a book and try to promote it to people who wanted to skip being victims to the system. I wanted to help them find ways they can change and grow. So, I went and did it. You can go out and do whatever it is you want to do, but the most important steps are to block out all the noise and to simply take action. You may have family members and friends that laugh at your ambitions. That should only make you want to go out and achieve your goals even more. Stop letting others control your life and make the change to help yourself.

Take control of what you want to do. We live in a time where you can create and choose to do almost anything you please. Back in the day, people did not have the freedom and options you do. You can create an app, make a YouTube channel, write a book (and self-publish it), start a business, etc. The list does not end. You live in a very special time, and if you use your time to your advantage you will only see wonders. If you want to start a podcast, blog, channel, business, then go and do it. You are the only one that's stopping you. If you tell yourself you are going to do it later in life, you most likely won't. If you made an excuse not to start now, as life goes on it will only get tougher to start. More problems will come tumbling your way. When you are older you will continue to make excuses because now you have bigger problems and your excuses begin to grow as well. Before you know it, you will be older. The only thing you will feel is regret, and you will continue to tell yourself excuses as you age. The worst feeling in life is regret! Follow what your gut is telling you and go out and simply do it. TAKE ACTION...

Chapter 3: Getting Started

Showing Up

The first thing you need to do is show up. That is a big percentage of the job. Just show up every day mentally and physically, ready to work. If you are not ready to work and mentally prepared, then you will find yourself on the short end. You will find yourself lost and you will start to tell yourself that you are not getting anything done and you are not going anywhere. You need to have guidelines for what you are going to do every day. It's almost like when you were working for someone behind a desk. You had things placed out for you to follow. Make a schedule and follow it every day for yourself. If you are starting a business, know what your next move is going to be. Always be ahead of the game and have your tasks laid out.

If you don't show up every day ready to work, you will start to listen to the negative side of your inner voice. Your inner voice will tell you that you are not good enough and what you are trying to do is way too difficult. Don't worry, everyone has that inner voice and everyone has a choice either to listen to it or to fight it. Your inner voice will not go away until you learn how to battle it and control it. Even then, you'll hear that voice from time to time; it never fully goes away. You have to battle it and tell yourself you can accomplish anything you put your mind to.

Being Disciplined

Without real self-discipline there is no such thing as true success. If you do not discipline yourself, you will find yourself in the deep end of situations instead of the person who is supposed to be controlling them. Discipline is a big factor when it comes to being your own boss. Discipline is what will help you have a clear mind and a mind that's ready to work. If you are not disciplined, you will find yourself in situations that are pulling you away from the goals you are trying to achieve. You will find yourself hanging around people who are going to bring you down instead of lifting you up. You will find yourself in places that have nothing to do with growing yourself and working on your ambitions.

As I mentioned in Chapter 2, learn to say "no." You should not feel bad saying "no" to going out with your friends if you are not where you want to be in life. If they are friends who are going to hold a grudge and get upset, then they aren't real friends. They should understand that you are trying to change your life around, and you are working on yourself and your goals. Take that step and you will see your world change. You will start to realize how much time you wasted each and every day being unproductive and just getting by. Life will not hand you gifts. If anything, life will hand you hardships and you have to fight through them. That's when discipline falls into place. You need to be disciplined when things go wrong. If you throw a tantrum or mentally break down, you will only hurt yourself, your business, or whatever it is that you are trying to do.

No one will be able to help to discipline you, except yourself. It all falls into your hands if you want to be able to stay cool and collected in moments that make you want to go crazy. We are all human and we have moments where we may not care about the consequences. We end up expressing our anger in the wrong ways. But if you were to do that at a business meeting you could lose clients and/or workers. Even worse, you could lose your business. All for not being disciplined, you could lose everything overnight that you spent years building up. If you were disciplined, you would find a solution to the problem and find your way around it. When you are your own boss or working on becoming your own boss, you will face problems every day and it's all up to you how you react to them. You would be able to react more professionally if you had great self-discipline. Stay focused and really take the time to work on yourself, along with your self-discipline. If you are someone who has trouble, then start meditating. If you don't go to the gym, start going to the gym.

Being Motivated

No one is going to motivate you like you can motivate yourself. You need to motivate yourself every day. I like to motivate myself every morning by working out, praying, and meditating before I attack my day. Start waking up early, hit the gym, and then get to your day's work. It will make a world of difference. If you drag yourself out of bed and then go to work, your mood will be all over the place. If you start your day motivated, you will have a good day. Everything I am saying is mandatory if you decide to quit school or leave your job because you are now in your own world. You do not have a boss hovering over you, making sure you get all your work done. You are your own boss if you leave your job. Sounds cool. But you'll realize how hard it is when you get the freedom to be your own boss. You need to learn to be disciplined and manage your time efficiently throughout the day. You are now free; no one is going to stop you from doing anything. You can spend the whole day watching Netflix and no one will know except you.

This is when motivation has to help you get started. When you are first starting something, it will not be easy and things most likely will not go your way. You need to have a positive mindset and you need to keep pushing. Something that will help tremendously is motivation. So keep yourself motivated throughout the day and keep pushing for whatever it is you want to do.

Motivation is an emotion that helps people take

action. You should not take motivation lightly. It can affect your production when taken for granted. You are either motivated by what you have to gain or what you have to lose. Motivation is a tricky thing to corral. Not many people obtain motivation or realize what motivation can do for you.

Motivation is what will drive you toward your goal. Motivation will help build determination, and you will not let anyone stop you from getting to the goal you want to achieve. It's very easy for someone to be motivated when they are first starting something or thinking about starting something. It's fresh in their mind and they are only thinking about good things. Which is great, but what happens over time is that the idea or vision they had starts to fade out. The project they started begins to get hard. They now start to slow down and do not want to continue or spend as much time as they were in the past, and that's due to a lack of motivation. The only way to stop that from occurring is to continuously motivate yourself and stay away from toxic, de-motivating situations. Demotivation can come from a negative family member or some of the people surrounding you in your life. In those situations, you need to tell yourself you know why you are doing what you are doing and what the ultimate goal is. Do not let others demotivate you.

Do not be the person that destroys their own motivation. Destroying your own motivation can come from telling yourself that what you are doing is too difficult and you do not know "if you will make it." If you continuously tell yourself you are not going to make it, you won't; it's that simple. If you continuously tell yourself you can do it, it will make a difference in your mindset and you will start to see the change that comes into play when you stay positive. Stay motivated every day through the good days and the rough ones. The more you motivate yourself and stay positive on the rough days, the easier it will be to stay motivated every day. It will become a second nature and you will motivate yourself without even trying!

Imagine you were at an office and you were working for a company. And one day, your boss walks in and says that you need to start getting more work done or you are going to be fired. How do you think you would feel and react? That job being your only source of income and the job that pays your bills. You would probably start working three times as hard as you were before. Why is that? You know something will be taken away from you and you will not be rewarded with a paycheck if you do not work the way you are told to. When you are free and you have all the time in the world, you need to do the same. You need to evaluate what your day, week, month, and year will look like. You need to motivate yourself like you have everything to lose if you do not make something out of nothing. Just like your boss would motivate you if he said he was going to fire you if you were not working to your potential. You need to tell yourself that or you will get nowhere because there is no one telling you what to do.

The best type of motivation comes when you have a passion to do whatever it is you are doing or planning on doing. People develop a higher level of drive when they have passion for their work. People who hate their job tend to have less motivation, but the person who does what they love for a living usually has massive motivation and is a lot happier. There are people out there who make tons of money but are not happy. Then there are people who make average amounts of money but are living happy and stress free. Why is that? The person making all that money can have a job that pays well but does not suite their lifestyle and they hate it but will never leave due to the salary they make. The person who makes less wakes up happy and goes to sleep happy because they have a passion for what they do and love it. Motivate yourself to live the life you see yourself living and start to pursue it. It will not happen overnight and it may take longer than you think, but work at it one day at a time and you will only see better days to come.

Having a Solid Plan

Have a solid plan on what it is you want to do. Do not tell yourself you don't want to attend college or you want to leave the job you are at, just to see where life takes you, hoping something will come along the way. That is not how the world works, you will end up right back where you left off in life or possibly somewhere even worse. Start game planning about what you want to do. Spend days on end researching the field you want to get into. Check if what you are trying to do is in demand and make sure it's something that's reliable as well. Really do your homework before jumping into something. Will what you are doing definitely work out? Maybe not, but that could be one of the lessons you need to learn before moving on to the next steps in your life. You need to take your losses and turn them into lessons. You need to learn from them and move onto your next step in life. Don't just sit there and dwell on your losses. What has happened has already happened. Now it's time to move on and grow from the experience. You need to learn before you can earn, there is no way around it. If you earn before you learn you will most likely not know how to maintain and invest what you have gained in effective ways.

Draw up what it is you want to do and really ask yourself if you see yourself doing it for a long time. Ask yourself if it's going to make you happy and if it's going to help you grow for the better as an individual. Do not hesitate once you have a vision and a plan, and once you are motivated to achieve your ambitions. You need to go out and make the jump. There is not a single successful person that did not take a risk to get where they are today. They got out of their comfort zone and made a jump. This life is too short, and if you are caught up in trying to live it the safest way possible, you will be left behind when it comes to freedom and happiness.

Executing the Plan

Once you have a plan, it's time you execute it! This is the fun part; you are now about to do what you've always wanted to do. You have knowledge about it. You are backed up, and you have the mindset that you are going to achieve big things. Just believing is such a big factor when it comes to following your vision. You had the vision. And that's your vision and no one else's, so why not go out and obtain it? We live in a vital time; there is no ceiling in the potential for individuals today. We have all the resources to create something and bring it into the world. We have everything put on a platter for us. The majority of us are blind to see what is on the table for the taking. I believe in everyone who reads this book. I really do, and the reason is that you took the time out of your day to pick this book up and read it. You had the option to do so and you chose to read it; not many people take that option.

You are one among many, and since you took the initiative to read this book, you need to be the one out of the few that take the initiative to make the change you want to see. There is no reason for you not to believe in yourself. It's time you put the plan that you have to use, and then go out and help the world see your vison. You have your own particular attributes that you can bring to the world and make an impact. If you are someone trying to make an impact, do you have to touch millions of lives to change the world? Of course not. If you touch one life you have changed their world, and you are making an impact in the world. You do not need to be an icon to change the world; you just have to be willing to make a difference.

If you are someone trying to bring a product or service to the world, you need to just go out and execute the plan you have. If you fail, you need to learn from the failure and pick yourself up and keep trying. If you wanted to invent something and you've tried it 50 times, it can be tough. But it just takes one of those 50 times to succeed, and then everything changes. You failed all those times but the one success changed your life. What if you had stopped at 49 and said, "There's no way I'm going to make it." And at 50 you were supposed to see your idea make an impact and really take off. You just gave up everything for nothing due to doubts in your head and letting failure overcome you.

Keeping the Momentum Going

If the plan that you have drawn up works, you will feel a great rush of self-accomplishment and you will love yourself for making the jump and taking the risk. But this is where many people go wrong. People who start to see results and success tend to slow down after the success comes their way. They tend to soften up and not attack their day like they did when they were financially struggling and the situation they are in is nothing but a goal and dream they wanted to obtain.

Many young people who see success tend to fall off because they start to slow down their work ethic and they start to enjoy the world and what it contains instead of producing the way they were for the world before things started to come their way. You cannot expect to slow down when things finally start to come together. There is nothing wrong with enjoying life and doing adventurous stuff once in a while, but if you are spending all the money you are making, then you are going backwards instead of growing. You will find yourself on the wrong side of things once again. You will start to slow down your work, which will cause you to have a decrease in production, which will bring fewer clients/customers, which will convert to your business taking a big hit. It's a simple draw-out, but it's a trap many people fall into.

You have to keep attacking your day like things never changed. You had a drive when you were stuck on the wrong side of life and now that you've seen a little bit of light you decide to slow down. That is not the way to go about things. There are many people who have fallen into that trap; don't let that be you. If you find a way to make a living, and are happy at the same time, do not jeopardize it by making irrational decisions. Are you going to be perfect from that point on? No, that's impossible. There is no such thing as a perfect person. But you can make your choices on your own and no one should be making them for you. If you have a clear mindset and are always looking to grow and improve, then you most likely will not run into this problem. Do not slow down for anything. The success you will start to see should only make you hungry for more.

Being successful is good and it makes you feel great, but what is true success? True success consists of being happy, having a loving family, and being a difference maker. Only then comes the financial benefits. People think money comes first and that's what destroys them in the long run. If you are a grumpy, selfish person when you are broke, then when you get money it will only amplify your characteristics. When you work just for money you will start to realize that money does not bring true contentment to your life. Sure, it can buy you fancy things, but it will not bring you the happiness your loved ones can bring. It can never beat the feeling you get when you do charitable acts. When someone is only thinking about money and nothing else, they will destroy themselves. The momentum they had towards becoming successful will start to slow them down and they will become self-destructive. Don't let this be you!

Giving Back

When God blesses you with special abilities in life, and you are seeing big results in all aspects of life, GIVE BACK! I'm not saying give every penny you make back, but you need to realize how many people are suffering in the world, and you need to realize how lucky you are to be in the situation you are in. Yes, you worked for it, but a million and one things could have gone wrong that didn't. Things you could not control. For you to have made it that far and have the things you do, consider that now it's time for you to help others. Don't be the guy or girl that doesn't help the needy because you think you did everything yourself and deserve everything you have.

The most successful people in the world will tell you that luck had a little to do with what they have achieved. If they hadn't had that luck, who knows where they would have ended up. Not all people are as blessed as you are, so you need to always think about what you can do to help others. You can help others in many ways that do not involve money at all. You can help people with your voice. You can help people by volunteering for something like a food drive. If you are grateful and give, God will only give you more.

Be someone who gives back to their local community. You grew up there and maybe some of the younger generation will look up to you and want to do the same things you are doing. This is something you need to always keep in the back of your mind. Try to help everyone you can. Do not try to make everyone happy, but try to help individuals and groups to the best of your ability so you can contribute to building a better world. The more you help, the better you will feel!

Getting Started

The hardest step is always the first one. It's almost like the first time you did something scary, like going on a roller coaster or cliff jumping, whatever the case may be. The first time you attempted anything like that, you hesitated both physically and mentally. You did not want to take the jump. You were way to scared and started telling yourself reasons you shouldn't do it. The same applies when first going into business or trying to pursue your vision. You will be nervous and scared. Your inner voice will start to tell you not to do it. When all of these symptoms occur, that's when you take the jump without thinking twice. You need to take risks in life in order to get to the levels that you are trying to achieve. If you want freedom, then you need to take on risks other people would not be comfortable taking. If you do not want to take risks, then have a good time working under others and being a slave to the system.

You may not notice you are a slave to the system when you first start working. As the years go on, you will start to realize a grown man should not be telling you when you are allowed to eat or go to the bathroom. You should not be told when you have to come into to work and go home. You may be in that situation right now and you may not notice it. Or you may be working your way into that situation without noticing. People don't realize it, but they are being controlled all throughout their lives until the day they die in the corporate world.

If you do not want to be a slave to the system, then take the jump. Before you do, just think about all the moments you got pissed off at work or in college because you knew what you were doing was not beneficial for your life at all. Once you take a few seconds to think about that, it will really make you realize why risking everything will be worth it. So now it's time to get started. Start following the simple steps that have been laid out for you. Show up every day no matter what, be disciplined, stay motivated, have a solid plan, execute the plan, keep the momentum going, and give back!

What is stopping you? Stop giving yourself excuses. Go out and make something happen! You should be even hungrier for success if life is hitting you with a lot of curve balls and bad situations. Instead, people like to feel bad for themselves in moments where life gets too hard. If you did less complaining and spent that time doing something productive, who knows what kind of doors could have opened for you.

It's now or never, get started! You will only see the years pass by if you plan to hold your idea or vision off for the next week or month. You now have the blueprint, so you cannot say no one ever told you. If you do not believe me or want to listen to anything I am saying, go and read other books on changing and improving yourself. Watch videos on the same topic. You will be told the same things over and over again. At the end of the day it will be up to you if you want to make the change. So get started now, do not delay it any more than you already have.

Start to manage yourself better if you're running into timing problems. You have 24 hours in a day. The most successful people in the world also only have 24 hours in a day. The difference is they know how to manage, prioritize, and invest better than you do. They have problems just like you and I do. Just because they're rich doesn't mean they have no problems. If anything, they probably have more problems than you think. Stop holding back and get started! Take that initial step and the rest will follow. You will see doors open for you and things will happen that you never thought would. You will meet people along the way who are the right people. You will observe and learn from them and they will help you grow tremendously. The only thing you have to do is get started. Follow the simple steps you read previously. It may not work in that order for everyone. But if you put yourself out there, you will start to see a change in the way you live and the way you think.

Grab a piece of paper and a pen and take a moment right now to write down the steps we covered and what your plan will be. Start to write your ideas down. Writing things down will change everything for the better. Your brain is almost like a hard drive. It stores massive amounts of memory. That being said, one way to help store memory and keep it from getting lost is physically writing. Write your ideas and plans on a piece of paper and you will see your memory start to change.

I personally like to write on a think pad. They are a dollar at the local Walmart and it helps me through my day, every day. The reason I tell you to write on a piece of paper or think pad is because it's one of the key elements to growing. I will talk about organization more in Chapter 5, but this is a step you should start to follow right now. Your motivation will fade, but if you write down exactly what you need to get done and what ideas you have in mind, it will help you remember them and continue to get after what you are doing, even when you are not at your best. Get started now! Do not let a second more of time pass by.

Chapter 4: Focus, Determination, & Mindset

Start Focusing More

Figuring out what you want to do in life is hard, and it may take you a while to come across what you were meant to do in life and what you love to do. However, when you do figure out what you love to do, you need to be more focused than ever. When that time comes, you need to realize that you only have a limited amount of time left on this planet to make that vision and dream happen. Start to really gather yourself and get in a state of mind that you have never been in before. Start focusing on every action you take throughout your day. Ask yourself why you do the things you do in your day-to-day life? Ask yourself why you wasted valuable time in the past watching TV or why you did whatever it was you did that held you back from growing and evolving in life? You will never get back the time that has passed, but you can decide what you want to do with your time now and in the time you have ahead of you.

When you start to ask yourself questions like this you will start to see the results in your day-to-day behavior and drive. You will start to realize that you normally wasted a lot of time in the past or you have done things that may not be priorities throughout your day. This will make you adjust your day-to-day living and mindset going forward with your life. You will start to really open your eyes to reality and the way you spend your time when going through this procedure of just sitting back and realizing how you have valued your time in the past. You may not be guilty of this, but the majority of people are guilty of it. It's great to realize it now. A lot of people spend time in ways that are not beneficial, and they are clueless that they are wasting their time. Their mindset is so delusional that they think they are doing the right thing by killing time.

Age has no correlation to finding the true meaning to your life. You can be 15 or you can be 40. Finding what you love to do and are meant to do can take time and patience. You can, however, figure out what you like to do at a younger age if you sit and really do some digging. Ask yourself what you are good at and what you are bad at. But be honest with yourself. Then ask yourself what you would truly want to do for a living. Keep asking yourself questions like this until you come up with some real answers. Do not answer your questions in a way that will just make you feel good. Tell yourself the ugly truth if that's what it's going to take, so you can hear it for yourself.

All the points you have just read will help you find your true purpose in life if you haven't already. Once you have that figured out, your focus and drive will automatically increase. If you are lost and do not know what you want to do with your life or how to approach life, your focus will be harder to obtain. Without true purpose for life, you will only find yourself lost time and time again.

You will find yourself in a better state of mind when you know your purpose because now you know what you have to get done. You know the things you need to do in order to obtain your vision. That alone will make you focus on what you are trying to accomplish. In order to be focused, you need to first find yourself and determine your true meaning in life.

In order to start focusing more you need to change up your daily routine if it's one that's not helping you. On the list below are steps you can follow so you can start to focus more throughout your day-to-day living.

The following steps will help you focus:

* Have a daily planner
* Set goals for yourself
* Read books on what you are interested in
* Listen to professionals in your field
* Tell yourself you can achieve anything—do not limit yourself
* Meditate for 10-15 minutes a day
* Write things down!
* Have a time and place for everything
* Learn to say "no!"
* Isolate yourself if you are distracted easily

These steps are very simple and can change the way you focus. Without focus you will have a very hard time achieving success. Success consist of happiness, financial gains, spiritual gratification, growth and more! In order to obtain everything, I just mentioned. You have to have extreme focus throughout your day. The thing I love about focus is that it's all up to you if you want to make the change and start to focus more. You get to decide if you want to get stronger or not.

If you really want to see a big difference in the way you focus in on things, then start to cut down on all the different things going on in your life. Start to really do just one thing at a time. I'm not saying only do one thing your whole life. Take it one step at a time; finish one task or project and then go onto the next one. Once you start to do that you will realize how efficient your work ethic is on a daily basis. If you have five things on your plate, it will be very difficult for you to get everything done and you might mentally start to break down, getting nothing done. You might start telling yourself that what you are doing is too hard. That is when doubt starts to kick in, and self-doubt will ruin everything.

Determination

Start something, tell yourself you can do it, plan for it, and go out and execute! It seems very simple until one actually tries it for themselves. If only life was that simple, right? You can make it that simple if you just put everything in its place and don't complicate things. We like to make life harder for ourselves than it actually is and should be. We like to fill our heads with all the possibilities of what can go wrong before we tell ourselves what the reward can be or what we have to do in order to obtain the reward.

We like to be negative on ourselves even before we take on the task we are trying to accomplish. If our first thought is negative, what do you think the result is most likely going to be? You need to tell yourself you can do it. If you were about to go mountain climbing, and before you started hiking you kept saying, "This mountain is way too big, and the hike is going to be too hard," then how do you think the hike to the top is going to feel? You're going to dread it the whole time instead of working and enjoying your way up. You need to tell yourself that no one can stop you and that you're going to do whatever it takes to get to the top of the mountain.

You have to be determined like never before. Life will only give you more reasons to complain and moan if that's all you do. If you love life and appreciate everything you have and work towards something, you will only obtain more. Life will give you reasons to quit all the time. If you are not determined on a higher level, you will most likely give in and go back to the same mindset you had before. I was not determined, like I mentioned in my story. I was not determined after I started my first company. I was happy I started and that I was going to try to make great things happen. But I was all talk with little to no action involved. I was not determined and I was happy about the fact that I started a company. If I was determined, I would have woken up every day ready to work. Instead I only spent a few hours a week working and the rest just wasting time.

Being determined is one of the biggest factors when it comes to developing a work ethic and being motivated to work every single day. If you are not determined, then all the momentum you have built up toward work will fall off. On the list below are a few points to follow in order to stay determined throughout your day-to-day living.

How To Stay Determined:

* Have a routine.
* Practice self-compassion.
* Notice how far you have come.
* Think about how far you can go if you keep working hard.
* Learn to control your inner voice.

Remind Yourself:

* You are in charge.
* You have a vision to obtain.

* Only you can stop yourself.

These are just a few steps that can help you stay on the right path and remain determined. There is no one in the world who can stop you if you are highly determined to reach your goals. The power is in your hands to make the change and to keep striving. We have no excuse today not to work toward your goals. Having all the resources in the world at your fingertips takes all the excuses we have out of the picture. You can learn almost anything in the world you want from your laptop or smartphone. The smartphone that you use is more advanced than the first rocket that was sent to space. If you do not utilize the power that's sitting in front of you, you can't blame anyone but yourself for not doing the things you want to do in your life.

The resources we are equipped with today are endless. Having everything we do also has a downside to it, and that downside is that there are many more distractions. With all the social media platforms and the new technology coming out, we are letting ourselves fall into a trap. We are easily side-tracked, and we end up losing track of how much time we waist indulging in things that have no positive return. This is the perfect time to be different and really get determined. There are not too many people who are trying to be producers versus being consumers. Many people are just utilizing what is in the world already and are ready to consume what is coming in the future. You can be a producer not a consumer if you put your mind to it, and you can even start with social media, which is a perfect marketing tool.

Now is the time you mentally click yourself in and say you are going to make a change. You have the option to change your life, and you can feed the world your idea or invention for everyone else to use. It is that simple. Stop watching what everyone else is doing and start making things happen for yourself. Think about where you can be 10 years from now if you invest your time efficiently. Many people today are very addicted to watching reality TV shows and scrolling on social media when they can be doing something more productive, something that can help them with their day-to-day lives. Instead, they spend hours on end watching other people's lives, and they wish they had what the people they are watching have.

I can tell you this because I myself was someone who did it. I spent hours on end wishing I had what these people had. It was those hours I could have been working on my craft and what I wanted to do with my life. I could have spent that time wisely. Now, when I look back, that's time I will never get back. Truly, its times like that we regret the most. It took me a long time to realize I was not going to make things happen by just wasting time and looking at other people lives. I had to make the change that I wanted to see, and it was not easy. But in order to grow, I had to use my time more efficiently.

Social media is designed to keep you intrigued and

wanting to see more. There are scientific reasons for the way social media was built. It was designed to feed your mind and make you want more. You have an endless explore page that you can spend days on end scrolling through. But still you will want to scroll and watch more and more. When you are scrolling and watching all these things, your brain is realigning your dopamine levels and you are getting a short high from everything you are absorbing. You then want to see more and more.

Think about how many times the average person goes online and scrolls through their social media page. If people were to go onto their phone settings and check how many hours a week they spend on theses platforms, they would be blown away. If you are someone who indulges in social media, try it! Go to your phone settings and see your time usage for the apps you use for social media. It will blow you away. When I did that for the first time, I was in shock. I looked at the amount of time I was spending, and it made me realize that was time I could have invested. It's an opportunity to grow that I will never get back.

It's one thing to use social media for business and promoting your service or product, but to be on social media so you can see everyone's "fake life," it's just not really worth it. I say "fake life" because the things you post may be true and real, but all you are posting are the good things that happened in your life. No one posts ugly pictures or news about the bad days they had. Life is not the way it's portrayed online, but people like to live in fantasy land instead of waking up to reality.

We are the biggest consumers on the planet, as Americans. All we like to do is take in. We consume others people's lives, we shop, we eat too much, and we go on luxurious vacations. We love to consume and that's why the people who produce are the ones who become successful. There is such a small percentage of people who are willing to produce. What helps them get to that level is determination. In order to be determined, you need to focus in on your life and not everyone else's.

Without determination, producers would have spent their whole lives consuming instead of becoming producers. Sure, becoming a producer will probably be the hardest thing you can do in your life. Everything will be well worth it one day when you look back. The hours you spent plotting your idea for a venture you wanted to start will pay off when that idea turns into a reality. Those hours could have been spent watching TV or scrolling through social media, but you took the time out and really decided to go forth with your vision. Start to become determined if you are not already, and follow whatever it is you want to do. Let no one come in your way. Remember, only you can stop yourself!

Mindset

If you do not take anything away from this chapter or

book, please take this piece of advice and never forget it. Your mindset determines who you are and who you will become. If you have a negative mindset, you will have negative results. If you have a positive mindset, you will have positive outcomes. Now, really ask yourself what your mindset is like and what kind of thoughts cross your mind on a day-to-day basis. It really is that simple. It seems like such a simple method when I say it, but people really struggle to understand their true mindset.

If you have a positive mindset, will everything be set up perfectly for you? Of course not. But when you have a negative mindset, you are always telling yourself something is too hard or you are telling yourself you can never see yourself achieving that one thing. If that's what you think to yourself, then that's what you are going to get in return. No one is going to believe in you the way you can believe in yourself! If you allow yourself to adapt to a positive mindset and block all the negative noise out, It can help you be unstoppable. If someone does believe in you more than you do, that's sad. You should really take some time and reflect on why you do not believe in yourself. Start to build a mindset that gives you energy and the light you need to succeed in whatever it is you are doing.

Figure out what is making you think so negatively about yourself and your future. If it's a bad group of friends you have or you are in a toxic relationship, then get away from that. It will only help you grow and become the person you've always wanted to become. You were just not ready or prepared in the past. Now is the time to make the change. If you decide to hold it off a second longer you will just find yourself in the same situations. People have a hard time realizing it, but, without doubt, when someone has a negative mindset, they are just edging themselves into becoming a robot of society. You were born with a purpose for life. Do not sit here and end up an average person doing things that just make you fit into a crowd. Stand out and be the one to make a difference; create the change you want to see.

Your mindset is everything, and if you are not willing to work on yourself, then do not be upset when you are stuck in life doing the same things with no change or growth involved. You decided not to make the change, so now you are going to fit into society perfectly. Do you want that to be you? Do you really want to be a slave to someone for a few dollars or do you want to be your own boss and live on your own terms? If you want to be your own boss, then start to tell yourself you are a boss and that you will do anything it takes so you do not have to listen to someone's poor attitude 9:00 am to 5:00 pm, and then go home to your family in a bad mood. Life will only give you more reasons to be negative on yourself at that point. If you are stuck in that situation, find a way out. Do not live your life scared or worried about being safe. If you hate your job, get up and leave. Be prepared, of course. Have a plan before doing it. But stop living a life you hate.

The reason I know people hate their lives and have a negative mindset is that they are always grumpy. They wake up grumpy, go to work grumpy, and come home grumpy. They are always so grumpy that their face gets stuck in a posture where it looks like they are always upset, even when they aren't. They may pretend like they are not victims of the system, but deep down they know they had a chance to change and still do have a chance. They just don't want to make the effort to do so. They feel insecure getting out of their comfort zone. Unfortunately, people like that lose many years with the same mindset. If that's you, put this book down this second and write down what it is in life that you need to change in order for your mindset to change. Write down what it's going to take to make the change. Write down what you think you have to do to see positive results in your life and hang that piece of paper up so you can see it every morning until you make the change.

Maybe stay at your current job a little longer until you can have enough saved up to invest in the business you want to start; however, change your mindset around while you are thinking about leaving and starting a new life. If you leave your job to start a business but still have the same mindset, you will be in the wrong place mentally. You are better off staying at that job because business consists of bumpy rides, and it has many downsides you have to be prepared for. If you have a negative mindset, you will find yourself banging your head against the wall when controversial situations occur. It may seem like business is nothing but rainbows and sunshine on social media. No one posts the bad days and the situations that occur that make them want to rip their hair out. In order to survive you have to have a mindset like no one else. You need to be positive and ready for any situation to come your way.

If you are looking for an easy ride to success, do not step foot into the entrepreneurial world because there will be times where you are broke, lonely, and depressed. If you are not strong and do not have an uplifting mindset, you will not make it past the obstacles that come your way. Your mindset will tell you what type of person you are as soon as you really take the time out and question yourself. When I was younger, I thought I had a positive mindset, when in reality my mindset was one that was self-destructive. I was a selfish individual. I thought that was going to make me become successful in life.

As I got older, I realized that true success comes from helping others and making an impact in the world. You feel value when you help out in the world. Whether it's donating or helping people learn certain traits that they may not have. Spread knowledge as much as you can. I never thought about these things when I was younger. I believed making money was everything, and I believed that you net worth determined your success. Later I found out that people who made boatloads of money were often depressed and even suicidal. How could that be? I'm not saying money is not important, because it's one of the biggest essentials to freedom, but there has to be a balance. You need to know the purpose of your life and what you want to do. Giving and making a difference in the world has a return no amount of money can replace. I realized that the more I gave and the more good I spread, it all came back in return in multiples.

It was my mindset that I had to change because I believed money was everything, and that is a very destructive and a selfish way to think. I could have led me down a path where I would end up depressed and lonely. Changing my mindset altered everything, and now I can say I have the right mindset toward life and my goals. You have to realize yourself or have someone tell you that you have a bad mindset because your inner voice will always try to comfort you. No matter what your mindset is like, your inner voice will try to make you feel as comfortable as possible. Take the time out of your day and find out if your mindset is positive or negative. If it's too hard for you to tell yourself the truth, ask someone you can trust to tell you the truth about yourself. Be determined to change your mindset if it is not where it needs to be. If you already have a mindset that's good and will take you down the right path, work on it even more. You can always work on improving yourself. There is no such thing as perfect. Throughout the battle of life things will change. So you need know what your mindset is like and make the changes as your life evolves.

We are constantly growing in life. Having the same mindset can really hold you back from growing and becoming the person you always wanted to become. You now have the choice to become the person you see yourself becoming. So, go out and do it! One's mindset has to do with more than just the way you think. The person you will be in the future is based on what you read, the people you hang around, and what you listen to. Do not hang around people who will hold you back or bring you down. Surround yourself with people who believe in you and want to see the best for you. Always continue to grow, and never stop reading. Reading will help you constantly grow and will help you stay educated throughout your life. You will see constant growth in life if you are open to always learning new things. The things you listen to will affect your mindset. Make sure you know what you are listening to and what the affects can be from listening to toxic things. These are all factors that affect your mindset, and it's very important to monitor them closely.

If you are eating unhealthy and do not work out, what do you think your mindset will be like? You are going to be on the less motivated side of life. You will be less determined to get things done because of all the junk you consume. Your energy levels are going to be out of place. Have you ever heard of the saying, "You are what you eat"? That's 100 percent true. If you consume unhealthy foods, then your future will be unhealthy. You will have less energy and that will have a huge impact on your mindset. What you feed your mind will shape your future. Think about changing your diet if it's a problem. Learn how your body works. Look up foods and smoothies that will help boost your energy instead of destroying it.

Putting Everything Together

Now that you have read about what you need to do to increase your focus, determination, and mindset, let's talk about what you need to do before committing to something. Make sure whatever it is that you want to do, that you are doing it because you have a passion for it. Do not step into a project or business just to make money. If your main objective is to just make money and nothing else, you will find yourself very miserable. Make sure if you are selling a product or service, that you would use it yourself. Do not sell something you do not see yourself using. It will only make you hate what you're doing and it will kill your drive before you know it. You have to be passionate about what you do in life or else you will just be doing it for the capital.

Love what you do! If you have love and passion for what you are doing, you will only grow with time. The reason I never gave up on my brand and started my own company was that I loved the process. I failed twice, but the process was what I fell in love with. I love bringing products to the market that people enjoy and have great experiences using. When I see positive feedback I feel good because that's a product that did not exist before I helped bring it to the table. To me, that's an amazing feeling. And now that I am in the cannabidiol industry, I've seen numerous lives changed from what I am selling. People with anxiety, depression, migraines, etc., are finding relief in my product! It even helps fight off diseases like breast cancer, lung cancer, and many more. It's truly amazing, I love what I do every day and I can't wait to see what else the journey and future holds.

The world is in your hands for the taking and now is the best time for you to go out and make something happen. You don't have to be the smartest person. You really don't. As long you have passion and a drive, nothing in the world can stop you. Go out and make a difference in this world. Do not waste time just taking up space on the planet. Help the planet grow and change. When you do that you will see everything in your life change for the better. Give people what they want and in return you will get what you want.

Really take the time to figure yourself out before you dive into something. Once you figure it out, follow your gut and go for it without looking back. I thought I was going to finish college and get a desk job after my ventures failed at the age of 19. I thought there was no way I was going to make things happen, so I decided to give in and go the safe way. All along I was meant for this, and I was lying to myself at the time to feel better. My mindset was off and I was letting it get to me. I told myself that business was not for me and I put myself down in every way possible. That is one of the reasons I spent a lot of time lost and confused. If I had taken the time to really sit down and think about what I wanted to do, I would have been back on track a long time ago. However, I let my inner voice tell me otherwise so that I could feel comfortable.

Get out of your comfort zone and go make something happen. You took the time to pick up this book and read it. The fact that you made it this far tells me you want to learn more and you really do want to grow and make the change. There is nothing holding you back, you can read 100 books like this, but it's up to you to get up and decide to take action!

Chapter 5: Organization, Strategy, and Persistence

Organization:

Organization is the most vital part of business. Without organization you will find yourself on the short end every time. You will have a tough time being efficient at your skillset, and you will have a hard time keeping everything together. When starting a business, you will already have a million and one other things going on. If you are not organized, you will only slow yourself down and possibly take yourself out of work. When you are organized, you not only feel good, but you can operate on higher levels because of the clarity in your mind. Your mindset will be better and your work will flow a whole lot easier. I was a very unorganized individual when I was younger. After my first failure in business, I realized one of the major reasons things did not work out was because I was disorganized.

I will be explaining to you a few tips and tricks that can help you stay organized. First, do not get lazy when it comes to being organized. It may seem like it's not a big deal at the time, but when you need to find something further down the road and can't, you are the only one to blame. You need to keep everything in its place. For example, now that most of the things we do are paperless, organize your folders on your computer. Have a flash drive and back everything up that's important or save it in the cloud. Do not take organization as a joke; it will come back to haunt you. Keep your office or warehouse space clean at all times. Do not tell yourself you will clean it up later. That will only make you procrastinate longer. These are all simple things that will make your life easier. It doesn't take long to do any of these things; it's just about getting up and doing them instead of telling yourself you will do them later.

Staying organized is a vital part of success when it comes to the work you are doing. Get a big white board or a bulletin board so you can organize your tasks on it. If you have a white board you can write down what your daily goals are. You can write down everything you have to do in order to stay on track. This is the most powerful part of organization for me. I write down what I need to get done for the next day on my white board or a note pad before leaving the office. When I step into the office in the morning, that's the first thing I see. There's been a handful of times I realized if I had not written something down on the board or note pad the night before, I would have never remembered to complete that task. When you have so much going on it's very easy to forget things. No matter how smart you are, it may just slip your mind. It's better to just take one minute out of your day and write it down.

Do not be the person who says they will be organized in the future. If you are not organized now or not working toward being organized, you will most likely never be organized. You will always hold it off and tell yourself you will be organized further down the line. It will be a vicious cycle throughout life. The older you get, the harder it will be to get organized. You can always change, even when you are old; it's never too late. But as you get older it gets tougher. Your brain becomes wired when you train it a certain way for so long. To change at that point is not easy. If you are organized, good for you; if you are not, make the change now, not tomorrow or next week. Make the change today.

Only you can decide if you want to impact your life in a positive way, and it starts today. One thing I make sure I do every single day when I wake up is to make my bed. The reason I make my bed is because it helps me start my day right. When I make my bed, my mind is already starting to prepare for the day in a positive way. If I wake up and drag myself out of bed without making it, then it only makes me start my day out the wrong way. If this happens I usually start out with less energy, as opposed to me getting up and starting it off the right way. Being organized is a key to success. If you lack organization and you want to seek success, it will only make it that much harder for you to obtain it. Start to change the way you plan and go about your day, every day.

Learn to prioritize your tasks, when it comes to organization, this is a big key factor. If you prioritize tasks throughout your day, you will find yourself organized. If you do not prioritize, you will find yourself a mess, and you will fall behind without even realizing it. This is why having a planner and writing things down will help you stay on top of your game and be prepared for the days to come. Do not take organization lightly. When it comes to organization many other factors fall into place as well. If you like to procrastinate, then being organized will be a lot tougher for you. If you do not take care of yourself mentally and physically. It will be very tough for you to live an organized life.

Being mentally and physically prepared is a big factor when it comes to living a coordinated life. If you are a non-believer in organization, you will find yourself in situations that will drive you insane. When it comes time to finding something you need, you will be wasting time looking for it. If you had been organized, you would not go through this problem and would save a lot of valuable time. Never forget that time is one of the most important things. You will never get time back; once it's gone, it's gone. Learn to stay organized so you do not spend your day wasting your time. When you are organized you get a sense of relief, and that relief can actually help you be more creative and work toward your goals more efficiently. You have less to think about and you know everything is in its place, so your mind is ready for more. It's free from thinking about smaller problems. You have enough against you when you are in business, and to be disorganized just makes you struggle against yourself. Help yourself by being organized rather than defeating yourself by being unorganized.

Ways to Stay Organized

* Write things down.
* Have a daily planner.
* Keep your workspace clean.
* Mentally tell yourself you are going to start being organized.

Strategy

Organization is a key factor when it comes to business, but without strategy there is no business. You have to have a strategy for everything you do in business and even life. If you dive into business without a strategy or having a true game plan, you will only find yourself on the failing end of things. You may get lucky, but do you really want to depend on luck? Of course not, you want to have a good game plan and execute everything you possibly can to perfection. It's almost like playing on a sports team. If you don't have plays and a good game plan, there is no way you are going to win. You can be the most talented or skilled player, but without a game plan you will have a really tough time winning. The same thing applies in business; you want to build a steady foundation, almost like building a house. If the house has a weak foundation it will collapse. Same applies to business, if you do not have a game plan or you have a weak one, your business will collapse. You have to have a strong foundation for business and that starts with a good game plan and strategy.

Anyone can succeed or be on the road to success with a solid game plan. You do not have to be the smartest person or the most skilled person. If you have a plan, ambition, and drive to get something accomplished, no one can stop you. Do not let small-minded people hold you back; go out, have a plan, and execute. Do not think twice after you have drawn up a good game plan and you know you will love what it is you want to do. If you do not have a game plan, you will only find yourself struggling and wondering what to do next. Do you want to be the person who does not know what to do next or do you want to be the person who knows his moves two steps beforehand? Strategy is something that's involved in every profession in the world. Like I said before, sports teams can't possibly win a championship without a game plan and strategies throughout the season. Same goes in life and business. If you go into a big corporation you will notice there are teams everywhere that have objectives that they have to complete in order for the corporation to make steps towards success. If the teams do not have a strategy, they will have a tough time trying to achieve their goals.

The teams that want to win plan every game—they plan for all possibilities. They hold meetings, they draw up what they want to accomplish, they set milestones, etc. If they were to not execute and do those things well, they would have a hard time achieving their goals. If your goals are business-related, you need to have a strategy for everything you do. Even when it comes to day-to-day living, without strategy it's very hard for an individual to live up to their full potential. If you are a person who has multiple activities to do a day (which most people do) and you are disorganized and have no game plan or strategy, you will be a mess and will spend a lot of your time confused. If you know what you have to get done every hour of the day and have it laid out before your day starts, you will have a much higher chance of getting those things done. The reason is because you have a clear vision of what you need to get done and you have a goal to get it done.

If you do not game plan you may not know what it is you have to do next or you may forget. You may add things to do or take away on your imaginary list in your head. Life is to hectic that you will only find yourself less productive and lost at times if you go about your day without drawing out your schedule or game planning. The most successful people in the world have the same amount of time in a day that you do. There is no reason you shouldn't be able to complete the tasks you want to every day. If you are someone who finds themselves falling short when it comes to your goals and your expectations are not met, then start to change things up. Wake up earlier, write what you have to get done for the day. Do not find yourself wasting time. If you are not where you want to be in life, there is no reason you should be wasting a minute of it. Go out, have a plan, and attack your day. After a few weeks of prioritizing, you will see a big change in your life. You will find yourself being more productive and less lazy. You will always have something to do.

It will be hard for you to find yourself on the winning side of things if you don't implement a strategy into your daily life. Things happen that no one can control. But for the things that are controllable, you have to grasp them and know your every move. People do not magically wake up one day successful. They put in the work, day in and day out. I believe anyone can do it. You do not have to be the most talented or have the best credentials. If you have passion and drive, no one will be able to stop you from achieving and maintaining the goals you have set for yourself. I want you to start writing things down that you plan to do throughout the day. Write everything down from when you have to eat to what your work schedule looks like, along with what you have to get done at work. Stay organized and start strategizing!

Persistence

Once you figure out what you need to get done and you start to make a change in your life, you will need to start implementing persistence. Persistence is to have continuous action in spite of difficulty or opposition. Without persistence you will have a hard time staying consistent and on top of your game. It's great that you now know about the importance of strategy and being organized, but without persistence it will be very hard to continuously have the same drive and workflow. In order for you to grow you have to practice persistence. You have to know that every day will not be great. You need to know that every day will be different, and some days there will be a bump in the road that may set you back.

In order for you to be your own boss you need to know how to handle these situations. It is not going to be easy, and the way most people learn is through failure and setbacks, when they stumble across them. However, you may not have to learn through failure. You can possibly learn from other people's failures. You can see how they failed and what they did wrong and see what you would have done and what you can do if you are in the situation.

I failed because I was not ready for the bumps in the road. I knew that 90% of businesses failed but for some reason I had this belief in my head that I was going to run a successful business and there would be little to no bumps or setbacks. When the bumps did come, I was not prepared and I was caught off guard. The tiny setbacks made me run back to my comfort zone and I told myself this was not for me. If I had practiced persistence, that would never have happened.

Being persistent in your day-to-day work grind is crucial. It will be very difficult for you to achieve anything and do what you need to do to in order to make things happen in your life without persistence. The average person quits if they are not immediately rewarded for their short-term effort. That is what happened to me in the past. I was upset that there was no return within the short period I worked on a business venture. If I were to continue to work and fight through the difficult days, who knows where my business could have landed today. However, I needed to go through that so I could learn that persistent is a key concept to being successful in business. If you can learn how to implement persistence into your daily life, then you will start to build a mindset that will set you up for success in the future!

There is already so much that's going to be against you when you start your own venture. Without persistence it will be very difficult for you to last in the business world. You need to learn to continue to work even with the setbacks that occur throughout the journey. If you can't do that or plan to do that, you will set yourself up for failure and you will go running back to the system.

People who are meant for the system are the ones that are told what to do throughout their lives. They enjoy it because the burden of making decisions for themselves is taken off of them. They live a life where their boss tells them when to get up, work, eat, leave, and when to go to sleep. I personally could never live a life like that. We live in a time where you can be your own boss with ease compared to previous times. Today you can easily live on your own terms if you pursue your business appropriately.

If I were to do a survey and ask people if they would want to be their own boss or work under someone else, most people would want to work for themselves and do the things that they love instead of working for a nagging boss who takes full advantage of them. Not every job has a nagging boss. But there is nothing like working for yourself and living a life creating happiness, as compared to working under someone else. But the real question is what is stopping you?

When you become persistent, not only do you know how to be prepared and handle the bumps that come along on the road, but you start to strive for more and you start to have a burning desire to reach your goals. The best part that tags along with all of these things is that your confidence starts to increase as well. Everything starts to come together nicely, and it really does not take too much to make the change. You just need to take the jump toward who you want to be, instead of leaning toward who other people want you to be.

When all these factors are put in place there is no stopping anyone from the road to success. It may seem a lot harder than it actually is. Being organized will help you build strategy; having a strategy will help you be persistent. With each task completed, you will leap to the next without even really thinking about it. Do you have to do everything at once and be perfect? No, it will never work like that! You need to take it one step at a time and maybe start out at a slow pace and work your way up.

Start by doing one task, and then when you have that locked in, start to work on the second and so on. It's almost like going to the gym. You don't want to do everything at once, all in one day. You need to work your way into it and make it a routine before you really start to push yourself to the next level. If you try to accomplish everything on the first day, you will most likely burn yourself out and not find yourself at the gym again for a while.

If you put being persistent into your practices, you will be going to the gym even on the rainy days and the days you do not want to go. You will have a mindset that tells you that not every day will be great, but no matter what happens, you are going to push through it. If you do not practice persistence, then you will not be prepared for the days that will make you want to quit. Those are the days you have to be extremely prepared for because your inner voice is going to tell you this is not for you and that quitting and finding something else may be an easier thing to do. That is why I believe persistence is the key factor when it comes to being prepared to run your own show and be your own boss. You can be the most organized and have the best strategy, but if you are not mentally prepared for the roller coaster ride when starting your own business, then everything else goes out the window.

The last two chapters we covered are crucial to making the change you want to see. Life will not hand you gifts; you have to go out and earn everything you can while you can. Life is never easy and fulfilling until you figure out what it is you are meant to do with your life. Everyone has a purpose and reason to be on this planet. For you to go out of your way and read and research topics on how you can work for yourself and not be a part of the system may be a positive sign for you.

The fact you picked up this book should tell you that you do not want to work for anyone else and you want to control your day-to-day efforts. You want to do it and there may be something that's holding you back. You need to figure out what that may be and tell yourself this is the time in your life you want to make the change and not be a slave to the system. You need to tell yourself you are done waiting and that the time is now. Go out and find what it is you want to do before you run out of time and life passes you by.

If you look at the way the average American lives their life, it usually goes something like this. From the ages of 1 to 20, you have fun, laugh, "learn," and grow. From the ages of 20 to 30 years old, you work on the weekdays and party on the weekends, living paycheck to paycheck. Age 30+, you grow out of the partying stage and settle down, but you are not ready for adulthood because you have not prepared for it one bit and now you have no choice other than to be in the system.

You complain about your life and how hard it is with all the work you have, and then when it finally comes time to retire, you are tired, beat, and the life has been sucked out of you. At that point, you are counting the days to death because you have nothing else to do. I've witnessed this first-hand with so many people. It is something that helped me open my eyes to making the change I wanted to see. You may have witnessed it for yourself. From reading it like this, it really looks like a life no one wants to live. But that's the way majority of people are living.

I did not want to see myself fitting into a crowd just so I could be like everyone else. I would much rather be different than everyone else and do my own thing rather than live the average lifestyle everyone lives these days. If the lifestyle that we just talked about is something that intrigues you, then there is nothing I can say to stop you. Some people are looking for that life and that's totally fine. But don't complain when you see people taking risks, hustling, and eventually living life to the fullest while you are stuck in a cycle that's leading you away from a life of prosperity and freedom. You will never be free In that cycle and you will always be controlled until the day you die. To me that does not sound like such a promising lifestyle, but everyone has their own beliefs and mindsets. The choice is yours if you want to be free or if you want to live like a hamster on a wheel.

If you want to obtain a life of freedom and live on your own terms, then you need to shy away from the way everyone else is living and start to build your own path. If you do not want to clock into work every morning and instead, you want to live a life of freedom, then you have to be ready to manage everything yourself. It may sound easy, but when you have to manage things yourself, you need to wake yourself up, have a routine, push yourself, and get your work done. At a job you are given requirements, and if you do not show up to work on time you may lose your job. If you work for yourself or if you are trying to, there is nothing stopping you from sleeping in late and not working as much as you are supposed to. There is nothing holding you back, and that's why a lot of people fail and cannot manage it themselves.

You do not have the same structure that you would if you worked in an office. You have to custom-build that structure for yourself, and that's one of the hardest things to do. Making a structure for yourself takes a lot of action and persistence. You need to push yourself to wake up early. You need to push yourself to do more than the average person. If you wake up early and start your day, it gives you a boost in a positive way. You may not realize it at first, but when you wake up early and start your day, you realize you are working while everyone else is sleeping, and that alone gives you confidence and gives you the mindset of an over achiever. When I wake up at 4:00 am and go to the gym, I have an amazing day, and I have this momentum that stays with me throughout the day. When I sleep in and then get straight to work I feel lousy and less motivated.

Everyone needs to find out what fits their lifestyle best and makes them the most productive. The only way you can figure that out is if you try different things. Do not do the same thing every day if it is not pushing you to give everything you have throughout your day. I like waking up early, which may not be the same case for you. You need to figure out what makes your body and mind the most productive. Start to build habits to follow those rituals. The first thing I like to do when I wake up is thank God for everything, and I like to tell myself today will be a great day. That is just in the first few seconds of waking up. That is something that gets my mind ready for the day, whether it's going to be a good day or a bad one. I know I started my day off right and that I started my day with positive vibes. If I were to wake up and drag myself out of bed, I would start my day with negative energy and that would cause me to have an unfulfilling day.

Find what it is you like to do and what makes you strive to have an amazing day. If you do not already have a ritual you follow, try different things every day for a week or two and see what makes you work to your full potential. Once you figure out what it is that gives you positive energy in the morning and throughout your day, apply that to your everyday life, no matter what is going on in your life. You may not be a morning person, but you will never find out unless you wake up early for yourself and not for your boss because you are conditioned to do that. Maybe you need more sleep in order for you to have greater focus to produce better work. That's ok, not everyone can sleep only five hours a night, but you need to know exactly how your body and mind work and how much sleep you really need. Albert Einstein said he slept for 10 hours a night because he was more productive and had energy to do more. Everyone is different and no one will have the same exact routine. In order for you to find yours, you need to really test your body and mind to see what suits you best. Just try it, you never know what good may come from it.

Chapter 6: Invest, Invest & Reinvest

Knowing what investing is and how to invest is everything when it comes to being your own boss and running your own business. When you work for yourself you can be making a ton of money one year and little to nothing the next due to a situation that may occur that makes your business come tumbling down. Sales can look magical one year and the next year no one wants anything to do with your product or service. You have to know how to invest your money. You will not be earning a steady paycheck, so you need to know how to manage and invest the money you make.

There is a reason many professional athletes and music artists go bankrupt after making millions. They do not grow the money they earn; instead, they live a "baller" lifestyle buying exotic cars with cash and not realizing that their career is not going to last very long. You need to know that anything can go wrong in business at any moment, and you need to be backed up just in case things do not go as planned. You also want to have multiple sources of income coming in so you can feed off of all of them and not expect one business to fund everything. You can spend years on end building a business and lose it overnight. If you spend your earnings instead of investing it will come back to haunt you in the long run, and it always does.

Not everything is about money, but when running a

business, you need to count every penny and make every penny count. You cannot live a careless lifestyle when it comes to your funds and hope to run a healthy business that's going to nurture you and your family for the rest of your life. You need to build a business almost like a building a house. You need to build it from the ground up.

You need to put everything into it in the beginning and really make a sturdy foundation so it does not come crashing down in the years to come. If you build a weak foundation the house will collapse and everything will come crashing down. But if you build the house from cinder blocks and really take your time and effort building it in the beginning phase, no storm can take it out. If you look online and on social media today, you will come across a lot of "one hit wonders." They found a way to make a lot of money really quick and are living a high maintenance lifestyle while not being fully backed up.

Instead of really growing what they have earned, they are spending their money on a lot of expensive things like cars, watches, and clothes. They are not thinking about the future; they are just trying to maintain a lifestyle they truly cannot afford. They are living a "keeping up with the Joneses" lifestyle. Today, it's worse than ever. Before, people would compete with their neighbors. Now people are competing with individuals throughout the world on social media.

What goes around comes around, and if you spend your life allocating your money to liabilities rather than investing in assets you will find yourself on the short end. A liability is something you spend your money on that gives you no return and is a debt to you. An asset is something you invest in that will give you a return; it is something that holds value that will bring you a profit in the future. A simpler way to look at it is that assets will increase your wealth while liabilities cost you money.

Liabilities	Assets
Cars	Real Estate
Luxury Clothes, Watches, Jewelry, etc.	Stocks, Bonds, ETF's
Latest Technology	Business

These are just a few examples of what liabilities are versus assets. Many people have a false understanding when it comes to the differences. Many people live their lives trying to be rich by looking and feeling rich, but they do not carry any assets. This is a trap many people fall into, and a lifestyle like that can be very toxic. I sometimes notice at a mall or a store there are retail workers wearing $350 shoes while working a $10/hour job. I scratch my head and wonder what they were thinking when they made this decision. What I came to realize was that they are working hard to just stay afloat amid everything that's going on around them. They are trying to stay up to date with the latest trends so they can fit in with the crowd. But what they may not realize is that they spent three paychecks to pay for those sneakers, and they could have invested that money and really turned it around for *double* or *triple* the money they wasted.

Not only do kids make these poor choices, but adults

do tool. Adults may make worse decisions than the youth. When you look at the way some people are living, it's very scary. When you see a grown man living paycheck to paycheck, who has a family, it becomes terrifying to just see how he landed there. You wonder how he handles his finances. There are people in the world who are less fortunate. But to live in America, there are endless opportunities for a better life. To see people piss away their lives and time is ghastly in my opinion.

What's even worse is to hear people complain about why their life is the way it is. They complain about how much they make or what happened to them in the past that messed them up from getting them to where they wanted to go in life. Everyone has their own issues and problems; there is no one perfect in the world. The difference between successful people in the world or the people headed to success is they do not let excuses get in the way or slow them down.

People can sob and tell their sad story about why they could not achieve their goals in life, but the sad reality is that they most likely wasted their time and took it for granted. People forget that investments are what will bring them a return and help them grow their finances. Sure, money is not everything in life, and your life should not revolve around just making money and thinking about money. But money is what's going to give you the freedom to live the life you want.

Whether that lifestyle consists of a having a lot or a little. You need to know how to grow and manage your money. No one wants to see their family struggle financially. You want to be able to be financially free and choose what you do on a day-to-day basis. Instead, people are held up in living in the moment, and eventually everything comes back around in life. If you spend your time clubbing and spending the money you make on things that are not necessities, you are the only one to blame. Do not feel bad about yourself when you are older and you have nothing to your name and you are struggling financially.

When you struggle financially, it brings many other problems to the table. I'm not saying finances solve all issues in life, but there is a big upside when finances are not a burden on you and your family. The number one reason for divorce today is due to financial struggle. It's very hard to live a normal life when you are a slave to the system and you are also trying to balance a healthy relationship. That is one of the reasons I believe investing when you are young is the best thing to do. You will have money coming back to you and you will have one major issue many people deal with taken care of. From that point on you will just be growing if you reinvest correctly.

Learn to Take Losses

Before you even think about investing, you have to be okay with losing. Whether you are investing in the stock market or a business. You need to know you will have losses. If you start investing and think everything is going to be positive and never a negative, you are only fooling yourself. That's one of the fastest ways you can draw yourself away from investing. If you learn to take losses, you then will mentally know that it will happen and it's something that's supposed to happen. Many people have this mentality that if they invest money into something, then they are guaranteed to walk out with a big profit. The people who think like that usually invest into something once and then quit, not wanting to return.

I personally use to think like that and that's why my first business venture failed. I thought I was going to never see a downside and that every day would be perfect. Those are the expectations you cannot have. You have to be prepared for the losses, both mentally and physically. It is almost like preparing for a big storm that's coming your way. You know that things may get bad, so you do everything you can to be prepared. The same thing applies in this situation; you need to know things may not work out the way you plan, so you will have to prepare mentally for the setbacks. If you depend on everything to be perfect, you will only destroy yourself and your business.

If you have a hard time taking losses, really sit down and ask yourself, *Why is it so hard?* This is something you should work on before going into business or any type of investment. You not only need to learn to take losses but you also need to know how you can grow and learn from your losses. If you cannot do that, you will be stuck always taking losses and never growing from them or learning anything. Yes, you can get a return from losses. You can learn from your loss and know what not to do next time. This is a very big concept to adapt to because your whole life revolves around how you handle the ups and downs. If you do not know how to handle the bad days you will let your emotions get in the way. And that can destroy you. Losses should be lessons to you, not something that forces you away from trying again.

Control Your Emotions

In order to make smart investments you need to know how to control your emotions. That goes for business or any type of investment you want to contribute towards. For example, when investing in stocks you cannot let your emotions control you; instead, you have to know how to control them. If you make investments based on emotions, you will be on the wrong end of things every time. You have to do your homework and know what you're investing in. Then, when the time comes, you have to go in without letting your inner voice tell you otherwise. When I first started investing in stocks, I would randomly sell my shares because I was scared the stock I was invested in would drop. I would do that without even looking up any information regarding the stock or any reason for it dropping. I would invest in a stock without checking any technical indicators or readings on the stock. Those moves I made where 100% based on emotions, and I paid the price every time.

When you start letting your emotions do the deciding for you, it can get really ugly, really fast. Everyone has emotions and they are a part of life, but to let your emotions do the thinking and acting for you can destroy you faster than you can imagine, especially when it comes to investing or running a business. Have a reason why you are investing in whatever it is you are investing in or want to invest in. Learn how to be in control when it comes to the decisions you make. Be fully aware of the consequences of your actions.

If you sit and ponder why you did not go through with some of the ventures you had in mind, it probably had to do with your emotions controlling you. You were too scared to make the jump or something went off in your head that told you now is not the right time. For the people who are waiting for the absolute perfect time in life to make a change and do something that they always dreamed of, they will never find the perfect time. The time will never be perfect. There is no such thing as the perfect time in life! It will never be the right time to start a business. It will never be the perfect time to get married or have kids. There is no such thing as the perfect time for anything. There is the right time to do things, but there is no such thing as the perfect time. You need to make it happen and not let your emotions stop you from achieving your goals.

Learning to control your emotions when it comes to investing will help you make the right investments and the right choices. For the investment to be positive, it is not a guarantee, but when you control your emotions it makes your decisions clearer. When someone is able to control their emotions while investing, they will make better and wiser investment decisions. It may seem like an easy task to do, but controlling your emotions when dealing with investments is a difficult thing to do. If it isn't handled properly it can hold you back from making good investments that will eventually bring you profitable returns.

You will never want to take risk if you let your emotions control you. You will always listen to your inner voice that's telling you not to take risks or to indulge in things other people are not doing. Our brain is wired to protect us from being in harm's way. Before ever taking a risk, your brain is wired to tell you to take the safe route. Your brain will do anything to stop you from taking a leap or a risk that's outside our comfort zone. It's normal for you to not want to take risk at first, but once you get used to the idea of taking risk, and you have a purpose for the risk you are taking, you will start to see a big difference in your day-to-day living.

Once you control your emotions and learn how to take risk, there is no stopping yourself to getting to the next step in your endeavors. If you tell yourself you are going to do something but then you start to wonder about the things that can go wrong, you will only let your emotions get in the way and make the decisions for you. You will not want to take risk and you will always be frightened by growth. In order to grow, you need to fail and experience setbacks. You need to learn from them. If you let your emotions control you, you will not take a risk in the first place, and if you do, and the risk you take goes against you, it will stop you from taking another risk in the future. Controlling your emotions has a lot to do with the way you operate and the way you make choices. If you cannot learn to control your emotions, you will be self-destructive in most cases. Things will not work out the way you want them to all the time. If you let your emotions get in the way, you will only stop yourself from achieving success.

Take Risks

If you do not learn to take risks and become comfortable taking risks, you will never achieve true success. You will not want to change things around and you will only find yourself in the same situation year after year. Do you really want that? If you can say in the last 12 months you have made immense changes to get closer to your life goals and dreams, then you are headed in the right direction. For the people reading this and thinking to themselves that they have not changed much since last year, you should take a step back and really evaluate what you are doing and why it's causing you to not grow or change in a positive way. Reading this and realizing you have not changed should tell you that this needs to be a turning point for you.

There should be growth in every step of the way in life, and not just once in a while. You should constantly be looking to grow and change. You can have setbacks and failures, which are a part of growth. But to stay constant in one spot can make you grow old fast, with no changes at all except how old you are getting. I've met people who, at 45, feel like they are younger than most 25-year-olds, from a mental and physical point of view. The reason is that they set themselves up for that by constantly working on their craft and their lifestyle. Some people let others suck the life out of them while others sit and try to figure out how they can make life more accessible for themselves.

If you take a risk in something and it fails, that's ok. You should learn from the failure and take something from it for the next time you are going to do something. People think failures are bad, but failure is what makes a person really learn and grow. Without failure, it's really hard to seek success. The people who make it to the top without seeing any type of failure are the ones that fall off the hardest. If they see any major controversy they cannot handle, it is because they have never seen failure before, and for them, coping with what is happening can wreck them mentally and physically. Every successful person has encountered failure. You may not know their story because they keep it to themselves, but they did not wake up one morning to having everything set up for them. They built themselves to that point by fighting through the journey and really working their ass off.

Do not be scared of failure; instead, embrace it when it comes and learn everything you possibly can from it. You have the power to react to the problems that come into your life. You can either sob and put yourself down or you can make yourself stronger by using the lesson of the failures to grow. You can grow in ways you could not imagine. You will see doors start to open after you start to take risks. Even if you fail, that alone can cause more doors to open for you than you think. If my first business was not a failure, I would not be where I am today. I was running a beard oil company when I first started. My target market was already so limited, just promoting my product toward men with beards. Women were cut out, kids were cut out, and a lot of men were cut out.

I was limited to an audience who wanted the product. Now I run a CBD company, and it can be targeted toward almost everyone. Men, women, athletes, adults, kids, patients, etc. CBD helps everyone, from people who have anxiety all the way to people who have cancer. It is also all natural with no side effects. If you do some digging you will find stories on CBD and how it has performed miracles on patients.

If I did not take the risk and go into the first business that I did, I would not have learned how things worked and what to expect. Now I know what I did wrong and what I have to do now so that those problems do not occur again. If any problems do happen, I know how to handle them and go about them in the right way. That failure helped me and pushed me to be better. The biggest thing I can take away from that venture was working under my friend Murtaza and his older brother Mustafa. If I had not done that, I would not have learned any of the things I did. Just being around them helped me grow tremendously, and it was a bummer that our business had to come to an end. But I can truly say it was one of the best experiences in my life, and it helped me grow as an entrepreneur. At the end of the day, there is a lot that I took away from the startup we had together. Sure, there was a good amount of money involved and a whole lot of time, but if I had not taken that risk I would not be where I am today. I truly believe that.

If you have a vision, dream, or idea, please go out and try your hardest to make it happen. Just take the jump and give it a shot, you never know where it will help you land. Make it work out. If it does not, use it as a learning curve. You will only see more doors open for you when you take the jump. Do not be a downer on yourself if things don't go as planned. You are only what you think of yourself and if you think you cannot do something you never will. When I was younger I was like that. Even in college I would tell myself I could not make it on my own, and that I would just fit into the system and work for someone in the corporate world. I was on my way to being like that for years until I changed my mindset and told myself I was the only one holding me back.

After that, I started to believe in myself and stopped caring what other people had to say about me. It was at that point that I started to see the biggest changes in my life. You have the choice and you are the only one who can make the decision. Take action and take risk, without underestimating yourself. Everyone on this planet is unique and has the ability to do something different and change the world in their own ways. You are capable of changing the world, but you are the one who has to tell yourself that and believe it! No one is going to believe in you like you can. There are too many people in the world just getting by and fitting in. Your chance to make a difference in your life and the world starts now. If you are not willing to take a risk, you will be stuck in the same boat for a long time; possibly for the rest of your life. No one wants to just get by in life. Life is way too short for that and you have too much potential to let life just pass you by.

It has never been easier to get an idea or invention out to the public than the time we live in now. You could not go and post your start up business all over the internet 20 years ago. You can make a free website today at www.wix.com and spread your product or service throughout the world. That is just one way. There are thousands of other ways you can get your message across the board. Social media can be used as the biggest marketing tool if handled correctly! Instead, people are posting pictures at parties and pictures for attention.

You can use social media to your advantage and make your product or service go viral. We live in a very special time, and for you to just sit and watch the days go by is making you miss out on major opportunities. If you miss enough opportunities, you will end up a victim of the system, and I know you do not want that. There is a reason you are reading this book: you want to make a change! Now is your chance. Go out and take a chance. Take the risk you do not see yourself taking. Do something that scares you. Take baby steps, but work your way up and continue to grow. Do not just take a risk once and then never again. Instead, continue to take risks throughout your life. And never forget that one of the most quoted sayings: "the bigger the risk the bigger the reward."

Investing in a Start-Up

Before you go into debt for investing in a startup, you need to know the following. Roughly 90% of startups fail. Many people who begin startups do not handle it the right way and their mindset is in the wrong place. If you do not have the right mindset when first going into your startup, your entire blueprint will be messed up. You need to attack your startup in the right way and in a way that can really make an impact for sizable results. First off, you need to know that in order to get what you want, you have to give your customers what they want. If you offer a product or service and all you are thinking about is profits and nothing else, you will find yourself on the short end. Maybe it will work out for a short while. But for a sturdy business you need to make sure your customers are satisfied.

If you really want to reach everyone in the world and make your product or service known, you have to make your customers happy, wanting to come back for more. If you really take the time out to make your customers happy and satisfied, they will start to recommend your product or service to their friends and family. Do not think about profits primarily at the beginning. Instead think about how you can make your product or service unique among your competitors and make your customers satisfied. What are you going to bring to the table that's going to be different? You can offer better quality, better packaging, add-ons, free giveaways, and the list goes on. Many people go into business thinking they are going to make a ton of money selling something cheap and the results are going to be quick. Sure, there are people in the world making money off cheap products or services, but they are most likely going to fall off.

The last thing you want to do is be a "one hit wonder." You want to make your product or service suitable so you are able to have it around for years to come; in order to do that you need to provide value. If you do not provide any value, what makes your product or service so special? With the web as a reliable source to start a business, there are millions of people selling things online. What are you going to bring to the table that will make what you're offering unique and worthy of someone's time and money? Sometimes you have to put yourself in the customer's shoes and ask yourself why you would purchase the product or service you are selling. If you learn to provide true value and have sincerity in your business and your customers, you will start to see results. Once you start to do that you will start to get what you want in return.

If you are not willing to sacrifice time and money for the product or service you would like to provide to the world, it will never work out the way you want it to. When it comes to startups, you need to treat it like a baby. You need to nurture it, especially when you first start, so you can grow it the right way. If you make your startup your side hustle, then you are going to get side hustle results. If you give your startup everything you have, only God knows how big it can grow. You will only continue to grow if you give it everything you have. That is a part of taking the jump. If you do not give it everything you have and you have doubts about what you are doing, you will not succeed. It's that simple.

Your doubts will destroy everything and will make you believe what you are doing is not worth it. The startup is only worth how much you make it worth, so give it everything you have if your plan is to invest in a startup. You will not only be investing a lot of money; you will also be investing a lot of time. Choose your startup wisely; once you do pick something and invest in it, do not look back for a second. Give it everything you possibly can!

There are going to be really tough days and days you are going to want to quit. Those are the days you have to push even harder. You can never get down on yourself. What kept my mindset on the right track was seeing all the successful people around me and how many years they sacrificed to get where they are at. I would much rather sacrifice a few years to live better days for the rest of my life, and that's how I played it out.

The majority of people are doing the opposite. They are living their lives to the fullest now in college, and in their 20's and 30's, and for the rest of their lives, they are paying for that. When you look at it like that, it shows you the big picture, and it shows how overrated partying and wasting money really is. There's never been a better time to start a business online. Forget what everyone else is doing, and start to focus on where you see yourself down the line. If you are waiting to start a business, don't wait. Start it now. Do not waste any more time. Even if the steps you are taking are minimal.

I'm sure you have had an idea and while you were thinking of it, someone else in the world went out and made it happen. As time went by and you were just thinking about it, they were working on their craft. Has this ever happened to you? It happens all the time and it's a smack in the face because you know you could have done the same thing they did. This happens to many people because they are good at thinking and talking but terrible at taking action. Many people like to just talk because it makes them feel good and it makes them feel like they can accomplish things if they wanted to.

This happened to me in high school and I will never forget it. If I took more action and pondered and talked less, then I could have brought the product I was thinking about to the market. Know I see that product all over Walmart shelves. Now that I look back, it was something that pushed me. But in the moment I was very frustrated knowing that I could have done the same exact thing and made my product open to the world to buy. You do not want that to happen to you. So, if you have an idea, go and start it now, even if it means you are going to start really small. Starting small is a lot better than not starting at all. And always remember, talk is cheap!

Figure it Out

The previous topics are just some different points you can invest in. For you to truly enjoy your life and the way you make your income, you must do something you truly love. I really loved ecommerce, and seeing so many people around me excel in it pushed me forward. I enjoy what I do, and the journey was my favorite part—it still is. You will hear many successful people tell you they wish they could go back and really enjoy the journey to where they are now. The reason they want to go back is because during the years they spent struggling, they were just thinking about becoming successful and did not embrace the moment. They just wanted to get where they are now.

If you embrace every moment, the process will be a lot more enjoyable, and it will make the journey more exceptional. Do not stress over the situation you are in now if you are struggling financially. Instead, figure out a way to make a different life for yourself. Find a way you can acquire the income you want and be happy. Don't think for a second that just having money is going to make you happy. Learn to have balance and live the life you have always dreamed of. If you follow the steps and procedures taught in this book, you will get to where you want to in life.

Nothing is going to happen overnight, but if you start taking steps towards the person you want to be, whether that's financially, physically, or mentally, it's going to take patience and hard work. In order for you to really figure out what is going to make you happy and satisfied with your life, you need to take some time and isolate yourself. You don't need to listen to anyone but yourself. Ask yourself what is going to make you wake up happy every day and what is going to make you go to sleep happy. If you surround yourself around others, whether they are good to you or not, they are going to feed your mind with what they think you should do.

Do not do what others think you should do; instead, do what you want to do and see yourself doing it for the rest of your life. If you are someone who has not decided what you want to do for the remainder of your life and what is going to make you happy, take the time now and isolate yourself. From the day I was 10 to the day I was 18, I wanted to do 100 different things. I wanted to be a cop at one point, a mechanic at another point, and an engineer. The list goes on. But what helped me decide was really taking the time to clear my mind, isolate myself, really ask myself what was going to make me happy and what was going to make me the income I wanted.

I did not listen to anyone else. I even took what my parents and family had to say and put it aside. At the end of the day, it's your life and you should do what makes you want to get up in the morning every day with energy. If you have people in your life that do not believe in your dreams, it's their loss. Do not let them ruin what you have in mind for your future. You only become what you see of yourself.

If you picture yourself sitting in a cubicle working for someone making $50k a year, it's most likely going to happen. If you see yourself traveling the world and working for yourself, you will make it happen because that's what is always going to be on your mind. Do not settle for average. There are too many average people in the world that got caught up in the system and cannot find their way out. As you get older you start to have more priorities and responsibilities, which makes it harder for you to change. For example, if you are 40 and have 3 kids and a wife, it would be selfish for you to go out and drop everything to start something up. I'm not saying it's impossible, but now you are putting others at risk. There are ways you can make it happen. But if you start at an earlier time in life, you can set up your life and your pre-destined family's as well.

This is why it's very important for you to figure your life out. Young or old, you can do it. If you are in a situation where you have a family and kids, figure out what it is you want to do and start to do it on the side while you work 9 to 5. Once things start to click and you are making enough on the side to support your family, leave your job and give everything you have to your business. Will it take longer than someone who has all day to work on their craft? Of course, but you still have the chance to change your life. The rest is up to you. I see too many people dreading their lives, saying they hate their job. But then they are doing nothing about it. Now is your time, and there has never been a better time. So, get to it!

Chapter 7: Make Your Dream a Reality

Now is the time you can make your dream a reality. Stop waiting for something to magically appear in your life because it's not going to work like that. It never has and it never will. If you think you are magically going to live the life you want and have the things you want without putting in the time and the effort, you are mistaken. The people who are successful or are on the road to success, dedicate every minute to it. You need to learn how to sacrifice things, especially at the beginning. Give up going out on the weekends or wasting time watching Netflix. Instead, spend that time working on your craft. No one in the world who is successful landed there by following the crowd and doing what everyone else was doing. They did something different and that's why they got the results they did and live the life they want.

There is no such thing as being too old. In the time we live in, life is very fast-paced, quite different from just 20 years ago. At that time, you could not decide to be your own boss and run an affiliate marketing program that brings in 6-7 figures at the age of 17. There was no such thing as YouTube. You did not have the flexibility to do the things you can do today. You can start an e-commerce business today and within a few months have a complete online store that attracts thousands of customers, if done correctly. I'm here to tell you that age has nothing to do with it. You can be 15 or 50 and still achieve what you want if you put your mind to it. In my book, 40 is the new 20, I share how you can make it happen if you have the mindset and the work ethic. Stop making excuses for yourself and start finding ways to live the life you always wanted to. It is too easy to fit into a crowd and be like everyone else, which is why the system has so many people working for it.

Tell yourself that today is the day you are going to make a change in your life. Take the first step, which is to have your mind set toward what you are trying to accomplish. Make a difference right now from a mental standpoint, and I promise you the other steps will start to fall into place. Stop waiting for the perfect time. I'm sorry to break your heart, but the perfect time is never going to come. People like to build fairy tales in their heads about how life is going to play out. Instead of building the life they want, they just hope for it.

Stop hoping and start making a difference in your day-to-day living. If you want to see yourself living the life you've always dreamed about. It starts with action. Once you take action and you start to make progress, whether it's slow or fast, you will start to see a difference. Once you start to make progress, you will start to see results. Once you start to see results, you are going to get into a good routine, and you will create a solid work ethic. From there on out it will just be a "snowball effect." The progress and growth will be like a snowball going down a hill; it only grows and starts to roll faster. You will have bumps in the road and setbacks, but you will have a sturdy foundation and work ethic to push you in the right direction, no matter what comes your way.

Until you have that solid foundation, there should be nothing else on your mind. You should be spending all your time creating the foundation to your business or idea and not thinking about things like going out on the weekends, vacations, going to sports events, etc. If your life is not where you want it to be or you're not headed in the direction to where your life should be, then you need to really take a step back and isolate yourself. Get away from everyone and work on your craft. Isolate yourself until you figure out what you want to produce for the world. Once you figure that out, you need to network like never before. If you are a shy person, adapt to communicating with others.

In order for your product or service to make an impact in the market, you need to attack every avenue you possibly can. Before starting anything, you have to believe your product or service is going to make an impact on the world. If you do not believe in your own product or service, you will only progress with minimal results. Your product or service is going to be everything you make out of it. Reach out to everyone who is going to help you grow. Network and meet new people. Meeting new people will expand your horizons on everything. When you meet new people who are savvy in the same industry as you, it will help you grow tremendously. If you are stuck in a small circle of friends, you will only live a life of small thoughts and minimal changes. Do not neglect the people who are close to you, but meet new people who have a dominant work ethic or run a business that's doing well. I promise your life will change drastically.

Don't think for a second you will be able to do

everything yourself. You need to be open to expanding and working with a team. If you try to do everything yourself, you will only see one side of it. If you have more than one pair of eyes looking at what you are looking at, it will bring more perspective to the table. If you try to do everything yourself, you may be causing more harm than good. For instance, if you are really good at putting a product together and providing it to the market that everyone likes, you can't be spending all your time doing the other things that are required for the product to be noticed, such as making a website or working on SEO (search engine optimization).

You will have to invest in freelancers or someone who is good at that aspect of the project. If you try to do everything yourself, you will be taking away from your craft and will not be able to produce the best product or service that you would like to. Sure, you may save a few dollars. However, if you are not bringing the best product or service to the table that you can produce, you are only hurting yourself and your business in the long run.

If you do not want to face finance problems, you need to have everything in your original budget before starting your venture. You need to have a written plan on how much you are going to spend on all aspects of the venture. You may fall out of line a bit as you go. Things may come along unexpectedly, and that's normal. Not everything is going to go as planned. You need to have a firm understanding of how much you are going to invest and what you are going to have to do to be as efficient as possible.

Take as much time as you need at the beginning to

really plot everything out because that's going to be the blueprint to your success. I promise you not everything will go as planned and things will change as you go. But if you have a solid plan at the beginning, it will put you on the right track and will help you get started with a clear mind. If you just jump into the venture without thinking, you may be stuck with something you do not like or something that has little to no demand in the market.

Have a Vision

Have a clear, precise vision on how much you want to make and what you want to do with your life. Tell yourself the exact number you would like to make in the years to come. Doing this will help you believe in yourself and your idea before you even get started. It will also help you see a clear picture of what you want. If you are trying to make something happen, but the entire time you are thinking about it not working out or not making anything out of it, you are only fighting yourself. If you have a negative mindset, you will most likely end up with negative results. You have to be positive and have a conclusive mindset in order to achieve your goals.

Many people are going to laugh at you and think you are crazy, but if you put your head down and really focus on what you want to do with your life, you can make anything possible. If you are someone who cares what others think and it bothers you, don't let it get to you. At the end of the day, it's your life. Do what makes you happy and take the steps needed to achieve your dreams. Find true happiness. Everyone may have a different interpretation of happiness and that's fine. Go out and find what yours is.

For me, ultimate happiness is freedom. When I was younger I would see people in their mid-20's or 30's driving super cars and traveling the world. It looked awesome seeing them with these cars and seeing the places they have been. But what really got me excited was realizing that most of them had the freedom to obtain those cars and travel the world. They had time on their hands. After speaking to some of these entrepreneurs, I realized they work on their own schedules and got paid to travel the world. For me, I couldn't think of a job that was better than that. For you, that may be different. But it's up to you to find out.

Once you have a clear vision of what you want to do and how much you want to make, start taking steps that will get you closer to your goals. Start with small steps at the beginning, working your way up. If you try to do everything at once, you are going to burn out and will only hold yourself back from getting to where you want to be. Not everything is going to happen overnight, and the process may take longer than expected. If you are following the steps and are seeing results, whether they are big or small, you are headed in the right direction. Too many people, when starting, want to see fast results and if the results do not come when they are expecting them, they quit. Learn to enjoy the process. One day when you do reach your goals, you will look back at the time when you started out and you will wish you really embraced the time that passed. Enjoyed it instead of hating it and neglecting the process. Enjoy the process and work hard. You will start to see your vision being formed in front of your eyes.

If you have the right vision and goals, you will find yourself in a world where doors will be opened and things will start to fall in place. In order for that to happen, you have to be willing to change—you have to be willing to grow. Be sincere with everything you do. Do not be selfish for a moment. If you are running a business, you need to cater to your customers in every way possible and give them what they want. When you give your customers what they want, you will get what you want. It's as simple as that, and I will continue to say it. If you are just looking for a return without putting any effort into it, you will find yourself on the short end.

Faith

Having faith will help you obtain all the ambitions and goals you have in life. If you have no faith, you will have no belief. If you have no belief, how can you believe in anything you do or want to do in the future? You have to have faith in all the work you do. Not everyone has the same religion or belief system, but having a belief in God plays a big role in life. If you have no faith, you will find it hard to believe in anything you do because you are cutting off a big aspect of your life. If you cut God out of your life and the actions you make, you will only find yourself with less ambition and confidence in your work.

If you have no faith, either in God or yourself, how can you accomplish anything? A positive mindset is what is going to help you achieve success. Without faith you are cutting out almost everything that's associated with belief. If you have no belief, you will find yourself empty on the inside. At that point, you can have all the money in the world and you will still have trouble finding true happiness and success. Money does not define success and happiness; it only amplifies who you were before you obtained it. If you are someone who likes to help people, once you obtain the finances you will help and give more. If you are someone who is selfish, once you obtain the finances you will find yourself being more selfish.

Really take this and put it into perspective. The last thing you want to do is make all the money you've ever wanted to make and still be miserable. As crazy as it sounds, it happens every day. People who have enough money to fund multiple lifetimes over again are depressed, and in some cases are committing suicide. Why do you think that is? This is something you should take time to think about. We weren't put on this planet to just enjoy ourselves every day and have no purpose. Do not make finances your only priority in life! If you have a gift, then you need to use it to make a difference in the world for the better. Especially if you were born in a developed country like the USA.

If you are born in a country that's established, you need to take a look around and realize you are very fortunate. There are families being destroyed in many places in the world. There are kids who have no parents and nothing to eat. I personally think it's your job and mine to help the less fortunate to the best of our ability. We are so privileged: eating full course meals and having the freedom to do what we want, when we want. There is no reason you should be wasting a minute being this privileged. You can make a difference in the world. You may not believe it, but you really can. You can have your voice heard around the world on the internet with a click of a button.

Take the time to really figure yourself out before doing anything. Figure out what is going to make you truly happy and have faith in whatever it is you want to do. Once again, do not make money your main objective. Of course, having money will give you the freedom you want and this book is about how to be financially free and not work for a system. However, know your worth and do not think money is going to cure everything. Many people lose faith, family, and friends when trying to obtain finances. They only find themselves lonelier than ever after obtaining the money and freedom. Keep your morals in check and start living every day like it's your last from this point on.

Have Confidence

Learning to be confident may be a very hard task for some, while it comes naturally for others. If you are someone who lacks confidence or has problems trying to obtain it, there is a solution. Before I break it down for you, let me tell you, confidence is a self-fulfilling prophecy. No one can give you true confidence other than yourself. Do not search for other people to instill confidence in you. That will never work. If you want to be more confident, start to really focus on the following:

* Have 6-8 hours of sleep.
* Have a good morning routine.
* Look your best.
* Exercise.
* Meditate or pray.
* Read and do research.
* Set goals.
* Smile.
* Stay clean.
* Help others.

You want to have a good night's sleep because you will have more energy when you are awake. If you do not sleep much, then you will have low energy levels throughout the day. You may also experience self-doubt and have little to no energy to be as productive as you potentially can be.

The next one on the list, having a good morning routine, is a point that many of the successful people I've researched and met say it's the most important key to being successful, confident, and energetic. Waking up and having a solid routine can help boost your day. For example, waking up at 5:00 am, stretching, and meditating can help you start your day out the right way. The first 15 minutes of the day are crucial and can make a huge difference in the way the day plays out for you. You will find yourself in a better mood and ready to attack your day.

Next on the list is looking your best. If you do not look your best, for yourself before looking your best for someone else, you may experience a lack of confidence.

When you do not look your best for yourself it shows you are a bit lazy and lack a sense of confidence. When it comes to being confident, exercising is huge. Exercising helps you feel and look good, causing you to be more confident in yourself.

Exercising is a great way to start out your day and can be essential to your morning routine if you give it a try. If you are not in the shape you want to be, it may be holding you back from doing the things you would like to do in life.

This next step is huge in my life and has helped me tremendously. That is to mediate and pray. I like to pray and meditate every single day. And for the days I miss, I almost feel like a piece of me is missing. Meditating helps you clear your mind and can really help you get through your day a lot more smoothly. It can help you stay sharp for the obstacles that come your way. I like to mediate every morning for at least 15 minutes, along with praying.

Everyone has their own way of praying and meditating, so really go out and figure out what works for you, and please give it a shot. Don't just try it once and think it will magically change your life forever. It doesn't work like that. If you skip out on this, and don't integrate it into your daily life, you may be missing out on a big opportunity to change your life for the better. Try meditating in the morning for 15 minutes for two weeks, and I promise you will see a difference in your mood and confidence.

One very impactful way to boost confidence is to read and do research. If you are well equipped with knowledge, you will know how to react to certain situations and you will have more of an understanding on the topics you read about. If you read about something you are going to go over at work, it will help boost your confidence when the topic arises. If you go into a meeting not knowing anything, you might be lost. And that can really destroy your confidence. Also, when you read you start to feel a change in your life and in the way you see things. You will experience an immense change in your personal growth. The average person reads 1-2 books a year; a CEO reads 1-2 books a month, on average!

If you want to take your confidence to the next level, you need to set goals. When you set goals for yourself, you are automatically going to work toward them, and you will do anything it takes to crush them. If you have nothing written down or anything in mind you want to obtain, you won't push yourself. Just writing it down can help you get started, and it will build a vision in your head that will help you obtain it. If you envision things, set goals, and chase them, then anything is possible. Setting goals will help you build the confidence you need to chase and crush any goals you have in mind.

Next on the list is to smile. Learn to smile around people and always look and feel happy. If you walk around grumpy all day, you're going to kill your confidence and you will be perceived as an angry person. You will not be able to have the confidence you want if you are not happy or look happy. Learn to always smile when greeting people and while being around people. This does not mean that once people are not around, you don't need to be happy or smile. Learn to love yourself and be the best version of yourself when you are alone, and you will find your life changing. Your confidence will rise in no time. Many people who are always grumpy make it a part of their posture. It almost seems like their face is stuck a certain way and they are always grumpy, even when they are happy. Learn to smile, even when things are not going your way.

If you want to boost your confidence, then you need to take care of yourself. Staying clean is very important when it comes to your confidence. If you are a man, do not skip out on showers or getting haircuts. You need to maintain yourself in order to have great confidence in front of others. If you are walking around looking and smelling like a caveman, people are not going to want to be around you, let alone listen to you. Look your best for yourself and I can guarantee you will see a positive difference in your confidence.

Last but not least, help others! If you help others, you will be doing a good deed and you will feel good about yourself. When you feel good about yourself, you are going to build confidence.

Do not think for a second you will be more confident through someone else or only when something positive comes your way in life. Instead, take the time now to build your confidence and be the best person you can be by yourself. If you do the things that are on the list, your confidence will go through the roof. No one will be able to bring you down or destroy your confidence. If you achieve confidence this way, you are going to be setting yourself up for the long run and you will live a life you love and not a life you were beat into. If someone tries to tell you otherwise, you are going to know your self-worth and nothing will be able to stop you.

Some people try to obtain confidence by doing drugs

or being someone they are not. What they do not realize is that kind of confidence is only temporary. Once you crash in that situation, so does your confidence. You should always be confident no matter what situation you are experiencing in life. If you lack confidence, you should really take a step back and work on it. Having a lack of confidence is very common. For the time we live in, confidence can either make you or break you. If you are confident, you can reach the world through an app on your smart phone. For instance, you can open up your social media app and tell the world what you are selling. If you do not have confidence in yourself, you will be cutting off many essentials in life that can help you grow in every aspect of life.

If you are someone who is anti-social and lacks confidence, do something that scares you every day. If you are scared of heights, go on a roller coaster. Do something that will make you go out of your comfort zone. If you lack self-confidence, change your daily routine. There must be something wrong in what you are doing. Take the time and really figure it out. Once you figure out what is slowing you down or holding you back from being the best version of yourself, eliminate it from your day-to-day life. It's doing the small things like this that are going to help you make a change in your life. You are not going to magically wake up one day with all the confidence in the world. You need to work on it one day at a time. If you stay consistent, you will start to feel the change for yourself.

Life will not just change on its own. You need to go out and make things happen in order to see results. If you lack confidence you will remain the same person, which will slow you down from growing and making the change you would like to see. I wrote this book so I could help people become the best versions of themselves without being stuck in a system that controls them day in and day out. Take the time now to really figure out what it's going to take for you make the change and go and do it. Stop telling yourself you are going to do things in the future. Start taking action now!

If someone believes in you more than you believe in yourself, there is a big problem and you need to fix it. What helps me the most when it comes to pushing myself and being confident in whatever I do is that I'm my biggest critic. I will never let myself only put in half the work. If I do something, I like to give it everything I have. If it fails, I'm ok with that. I will gladly take the loss as a lesson. But if I give it only half my effort and it fails, that's on no one but me. Having confidence can help you push yourself to give whatever it is you're doing your all. If you lack confidence in a business you would like to start or idea you would like to invest in, do you really think it will do well? You need to have the confidence and believe in it way before it's something that grabs people's attention. If you are not confident about it, your idea will only become as great as you believe it to be.

Chapter 8: Time!

"Time is valuable, and when it is gone, it is gone. Time is wealth, unlike money, when it is gone you cannot replace it," ~Napoleon Hill.

Your time on this planet is very limited. A lot of people do not realize this and take it for granted. I'm sure you've been told multiple times in your life that you only live one life. You need to know that's a fact and there is no changing that. Unfortunately, people like to hide behind the fact that they have limited time on earth and really find ways to waste it without them feeling like they are giving up something valuable. A lot of people like to build this illusion in their head that they are going to change things around down the road in life when the time is right. Some people believe that they are living their life to their full potential, but in reality they are wasting half their time accomplishing little to nothing.

It's a sad reality, but it's the truth. Many people are not realizing they are wasting time. They need to know they will never get it back. If you have an idea or a venture you want to start, do not wait for the perfect time. There is no such thing as the perfect time in life. You will never find it; so stop searching for it. Will there be the right time for certain things? Yes. However, learn to use time for yourself instead of letting it be used against you. Everyone should know how to invest their time in a proper manner. If you do not invest your time properly, you will have a lot of regrets as you get older. Having regrets is not the type of weight you need or want on your shoulders.

You should be living the life you want to. In order for you to do that, you need to learn how to really utilize your time. If you can build your time management skills effectively, I can promise that you will live the life you want. If you are busy goofing around and not prioritizing, do not feel bad in the future when you are in a situation you do not want to be in or you are stuck in a system that you do not like. That is where the system or government wants you to be. That is how the system operates. It's a vicious cycle and you are going to find yourself trapped on a hamster wheel if you do not get ahead now.

You need to know that the time you have wasted will never come back. Let that soak in for a second. It's obvious that everyone knows that, but not many people really take the time to think about it. Think about what you have done in the last five years. Do you feel like you have spent every minute wisely? Now think about how fast the last five years of your life has flown by. Life is only going to go by faster, so you need to realize how important time really is. If you just live life day-by-day without thinking about the future, do not expect to live the life you dream about. For some people that's okay. But the fact that you are reading this book tells me you do not want to live the way you've been living thus far. You want to make a change in your life, and I'm here to tell you now is the time.

The time for change will not always be available in the years to come. It has to be now if you want to see results in the years to come. All of this sounds very simple, but many people live their entire lives wasting their precious time. When they get old and wrinkly they start to wonder what happened to the time. Do not be that person. It's too common these days. You were not put on this planet to be a robot or to just watch the days go by. You live in a time where you can make anything you want possible with little to no money to start. There is opportunity lying around you, right and left. We live in a time where not many people have a legitimate excuse not to be where they want to be in life.

It's sad to see people create excuses due to the lack of drive they have as well as blame others for their problems. Everyone in the world has issues. Nothing is perfect. If you are someone who feels sorry for themselves, I'm here to tell you to stop lying to yourself. You are only fooling yourself and creating an illusion in your head. You're telling yourself it's okay for you to do certain things or act in a lousy way because you do not have what it takes. Instead, think about how fortunate you are for having water and clothes to put on your back. That will put you in your place if you are someone who thinks they do not "have it" like others do. Sure, some people may be gifted more than others or may have things handed to them. That's ok. They may does not understand the struggle. Those are usually the people who can't deal with controversy when it comes. Some of the most successful people in the world started with little to nothing. Do not feel bad for yourself. Instead, figure out what is holding you back from getting to where you want to be in life.

What you are about to read may really make you look at life from another angle. If you live the average lifespan, which is roughly around 75 years, you are not really living those 75 years to the full amount.

Let's do the math on how much time you really have of those 75 years. Say you sleep 8 hours a day, which is 1/3 of the day, and you live to 75. You will have spent 25 of those years sleeping. Or, a scarier way to put it, is you will sleep 9,125 days, to be exact. It's simple math. But not many people take the time to think about this. 25 years gone, just like that. Eight hours a night is all the sleep you need. For the people who sleep more, the numbers might just give you a heart attack. Some people are sleeping 10+ hours, and then taking naps throughout the day. How are you going to live the life you want, doing that? No one should feel bad for the people who love to kill their time and not take advantage of it.

Say you sleep 25 years, if you live to 75. Now you have 50 years remaining. The first 20 years of your life you were spending developing yourself. That leaves you with 30 years. Say you work for 8 hours a day for 30 years. That is 10 years gone, working. Now you are left with 20 years! You are really *living* for 20 years. Let that settle in. What you do with those 20 years is up to you. Oh, and one more thing. You can die tomorrow. Not everyone will live to 75. You need live as if every day is your last from this point on, and I promise you will start to see a big difference in your life.

A lot of people are wasting all the time in the world from the ages of 15-30. Then when shit starts to get real and life really starts to settle in, then people try to change things around. Why not change things now so you can live a life you want and one that you have built for you and your family. It's time people start to see how life really is and how it plays out. Too many people are just sitting back and watching the clock tick while they are getting closer to their death bed. Now is the time to really wake up and make the change for yourself. If you are lucky enough to live to the age of 75, you better find a way to utilize those 20 years or else they will just fly by like the rest. You will just be "sleeping" in the years you are awake, and the moment you wake up and realize the time you have wasted, death will be right around the corner. It sucks to read or hear about this. No one wants to talk about death or hear about it, but you should not hide from it because it's going to come your way one day or another. So stop wasting your precious time!

Strategies for Using Your Time Wisely

* Wake up early.
* Have a daily/monthly planner!!!
* Have a firm schedule.
* Have a dynamic task list.
* Cut off the people holding you back.
* Know your surroundings.
* Quit bad habits.
* Always remind yourself there are 24 hours in a day.
* STOP PROCASTINATING.

Life is only going to pass by more quickly unless you grasp it and utilize every second remaining. Use the strategies above to get started if you feel you do not use your time wisely. If you are on the right track or feel you are headed on the right track, use this as a check list or a reminder for yourself.

When it comes to using your time wisely and really utilizing your day, you need to be a morning person whether you like it or not. Being a morning person has tremendous benefits that can help you get your day started and put your life on track. If you wake up early you will want to go to bed early. There is nothing more distracting than the night life, and what kind of slack it can bring into your life. If you're someone who likes going out every night, you should really consider waking up early and starting your day bright and early, so you can fall asleep at a reasonable time and stay focused. Also, when you wake up in the morning and you start your day the right way, it can have a huge effect on the rest of your day.

When you wake up early, that gives you room to exercise and read. If you can wake up and do those two things every day, you will feel a huge change in your life within weeks. Some things to do in the morning that can help you have a good rest of your day include: practice gratitude, pray/meditate, stretch, drink a smoothie/water, and exercise. These essentials can help you make the flip in your life that you are looking for. If you are out clubbing at 2:00 am, you probably will not wake up until at least 10:00 am. Along with that comes a hangover and a bunch of toxic stuff in your body. I'm not saying you need to become a robot and never go out, but you should know your worth and the value of the time you are giving up when indulging in activities like that all the time.

When trying to use your time wisely and effectively, you need to have a daily planner on what you need to accomplish. When I say a daily planner, I do not mean in your head. You need to write things down so you can have a checklist with you throughout the day. Write down what you need to get done for the next day. Know what you have to accomplish the next day and wake up with a plan ready in hand for that day. If you are starting a venture, you have a lot of time on your hands, and if it's not managed correctly, then you can fall behind. It's easy then to fail to find the results you are looking for. If you write things down and it helps you reach your goals every day, you will have created something I like to call a *dynamic task list*. That's going to help you get to the next level. Many people want to see big results fast, but if you take it one day at a time and really give it everything you have, nothing can stop you from achieving your goals.

Set goals, not only daily, but goals you want to accomplish weekly and monthly. Push yourself to try to reach those goals one step at a time.

The next thing on the list is by far the hardest for most people. Unfortunately, many times the people closest to us are the ones that are holding us back or creating negative energy. When you are being pulled down by others, you fall into a trap that can be very toxic. People who are negative and small-minded can really hold you back from getting to where you want to be in life. When you are around them you end up thinking like them. Their energy rubs off and you will start to take notice. It's almost like a contagious disease.

Live how you want to live and if someone is holding you back, let them go. If they were really close to you, they would want the best for you. They would not try to manipulate you and hold you back from achieving the goals you are trying to get to. This is by far one of the hardest things to do. If you want to really see a difference in your life and see your time being spent productively, this is a must. You need to learn to let people holding you down go. Know your surroundings at all times when you are out. Know what being around the wrong company of people can do to you.

Next, you need to identify your bad habits. Take the time out now to write down all the bad habits you have. Do not take this lightly. Your habits are what can make you or break you as a person. If you have a bad habit of procrastinating. It can hold you back from achieving wonders in life. Many people do not realize how much their habits hold them back in life and from working to their full potential. It is okay if your list of bad habits is long. If you identify your bad habits now, you can work on fixing them and fighting against them. People like to hide behind the ugly truth and don't like to think about the negative things they do in life. Take the list you make and put it somewhere you can see it every day until you fix and conquer the bad habits you have.

If you follow all of the things on the list and really pay attention to the time that's available to you, your life can really swing around. If you use time ineffectively, you can really turn things around. Nothing in this world can replace your time. It is one thing that's gone when it's gone and will never come back. You can always make money after losing it. You can always fix things that are broken in your life. But you can never go back in time. Use your time today wisely and you will see a difference tomorrow. If you sit and believe you will change things in the future, you are only going to be delaying what you can accomplish now. The opportunity may not be there down to road in life.

Take what you have and run with it. If you have an idea, go out and make it happen. Do not make excuses for you not being able to do the things that you would love to do. Instead, figure out ways to accomplish the things you want and make them happen. You can make the change in your life so much faster than you anticipate if you just take the time and effort to do so, instead of simply delaying things. We have 24 hours in a day, which really is not enough time. Everyone in the world has only 24 hours in a single day, so why would you expect things to be any different for you? The most successful people in the world do not have 36 hours in a day. They have the same time you do.

Managing your Time

Now you have a glimpse of how valuable your time really is. Ask yourself if you have used all your time efficiently to this point in your life? Everyone will have different answers to what they have wasted their time on, but a majority of people on earth have wasted their time on one thing or another. If you truly want to make changes in your life, then don't tell yourself you never wasted any time in your life or you currently do not waste any time. Instead, identify your flaws and try to fix them. If you are someone who likes to tell yourself you are perfect, you will never work on yourself or change for the better due to the fact that you think you are perfect and there is nothing wrong in the way you are living.

Learn to swallow your pride and dig into problems to find true answers. For instance, if you are someone who likes to waste time on watching Netflix too much, identify the problem and fix it. Do not sit there and tell yourself you do not watch too much T.V. if you sit hours on end every day and watch Netflix shows. That is just an example, but too many people like to hide behind their insecurities. Now is the chance for you to realize what you are doing wrong and turn it around. In order to realize what you are doing wrong; you need to stop lying to yourself. Sometimes people lie to themselves so much they start to believe their own lies. If you tell yourself you do not go out a lot, but you are someone who spends multiple nights a week going out, you are just building an illusion in your own head and believing it so you can feel better about yourself.

No one is going to feel great making a change for the better. It is something that's very hard to do, especially when you are stuck in many bad habits. There is a reason only a few people are able to do it and make the transition in their lives. It takes a lot of hard work, patience, and persistence. The fact that you are reading a book like this shows you want to see a difference and that you are willing to work for it. Do not take any of what you are reading lightly. The time on your hands is very limited and only a handful of people will get ahead while the rest stay stuck in a deadbeat system. Do not be the one to get stuck in a system that's going to control you like a slave and take full advantage of you.

Do What Makes You Happy

There are too many people living their lives today for others and not for themselves. Whether it's your parents, girlfriend, or spouse, you need to find what makes you happy first before trying to please others in every way possible. Do not live for others without a true recognizing the purpose for your own life. I'm not saying go out and be a rebel against your family and friends. If you get stuck trying to find happiness and satisfaction through other people, you will only find yourself more vulnerable than ever before. Do something that will make a difference in your life and your world. If you are surrounded with people who do not support you, then there needs to be a change in the people you surround yourself with. If you live to impress others and to make others happy all the time, you will not be living the life designed for you, and that will cause you to live a lie.

Be true to yourself and what you want to do in life. Having a false understanding of how things are supposed to work out in life can really take a toll on one's mindset and lifestyle. Do not think that all the money in the world is going to make you happy. Do not think the lifestyles of others that you see on social media are going to make you happy. What you do not see are these peoples' actual lifestyles and how they operate behind the scenes. Whoever posts on social media has control of what they post. You will never see people posting their bad days or situations that reflect negatively on them on social media. You are just going to see people posting their ups in life and not their downs.

It's very easy to fall into wanting what others have through social media and TV. The saying "keeping up with the Joneses" is a result of watching and wanting to be the neighbors that surrounds you, causing people to try to compete with the materialistic belongings they own and the lifestyle it seems they are living from the outside. Now, "keeping up with the Joneses" is on a whole new level. People are seeing others' social media lives throughout the world, wishing they had what they see on their phone screen. Not only do they want what others have but they are downgrading everything they have in their own life.

Find what makes you happy and fits your unique lifestyle the best, and I promise you will live a happy life. For example, if you love playing video games, aim to become a professional video gamer. Do not let anyone stop you or tell you otherwise. E-sports have grown tremendously in the last few years, as of 2018. In the years to come it will only expand and draw in more viewers and players. There are kids who are 17 getting $2 million contracts to play video games. When did anyone think that was going to happen? If you were to stand in front of an average 60 year old and tell them you wanted to become a professional video gamer, they would lose their mind. Times have changed and now is the time to do what you want and like because the opportunity is on the table for the taking and may not be there for long. The rest is up to you.

Going back to the video gaming, how many 15 year-olds do you know who watch physical sports like basketball, football, etc.? The young kids are the future to our society, so if they love playing video games and watching others play video games, that is what the future is going to hold. Do not think for a second things will remain the same for the rest of your life. You need to realize that things change rapidly and the world does not slow down for anyone. You have to constantly reinvent yourself throughout your life and grow with change. If you cannot adapt to change, you will be left behind. That's when you end up not living a fulfilling life.

Learn to think and create on your own now, so down the road you do not get taken advantage of. Find what you love to do and go out and make it happen, no matter how much time and effort it takes. No one on earth wants others taking advantage of them. But if you do not get ahead and have something going for you, it will make you vulnerable to life and how to go about it. You will have to work for people you do not want to work for and act like you are doing something that makes you happy.

Once time has passed it will never come back. It's up to you to determine what you do with it. If you want to do what makes you happy, you need to be willing to sacrifice things average people do not sacrifice. Whether you want to run a business online or open up a retail store or whatever the case maybe. You will have to change things up and give up the nights out and hanging out if that's something you indulge your time in. You will have to work like you have never worked before and take action on every opportunity you get. There isn't going to be anyone telling you what to do or how to manage your work. It's all up to you and what you do with that time. It may sound like an easy concept, but managing yourself is a very difficult task for many people because they have all the freedom and time to do whatever they please.

That is a big problem in the school system. As students we were taught to follow bells and raise our hands for permission, never really taking things into account for ourselves. Then as we get older we are told what time to come to work and how to operate at work. We are fed into a system that takes full control and advantage of us, and many of us do not even realize it. When we do get free time and have opportunity on our hands, we do not know how to manage it and control ourselves. This is a problem that many are facing, and it's slowing people down and holding them back from getting to where they want to be in life.

Either you take full advantage of your time now, or you get taken advantage of and lose out on having freedom. Once you are trapped into a system that commands how you live your life, you are stuck doing what others want you to do and not what you would like to do. Everyone wants to be free and live life how they see it, but not many are willing to work for it and build it. It's either you go out and make things happen or you sit back and play it safe. When you play it safe, you get trapped into working for others and living your life being pushed around. The more you look for safety, the more you will be lost. Safety is nothing but an illusion and you will only be holding yourself back from taking risk in life and getting out of your comfort zone.

Go out and do something that scares you. Stop searching for safety, whether it's safety in a job that pays a decent salary, or safety in the way you live your life. Learn to take risk and be able to handle losses. If you are scared to take risks, you will always be working for someone who is willing to take the risks you never did. If you are stuck at a job you hate, use the time you have on your hands and really concentrate on one thing that can help you generate an income and free yourself from the job you are trapped in. Focus on one thing when first investing in an idea you have. Do not think if you do five things and have multiple streams of income right away, you will free yourself up from work.

Yes, having multiple sources of income is a big part of being your own boss and living the life you desire. However, no one ever became dominant in their field by trying to do ten different things at once. They absolutely gave everything they had to the one idea and venture they went into and then after they established that one, they invested elsewhere. If you try to do too much at once you will not get anything accomplished.

A good way to put it is this. Imagine you were rabbit hunting and you spotted two rabbits while you had a bow and arrow. If you try to kill both rabbits at once, you would be stuck trying to kill them all day and night, probably never actually making it happen. Instead, if you killed one rabbit and then went for the second one, you would actually make progress and see results. The same goes in business or an idea you have. Do not try to accomplish everything right away. Instead take the time and really give one idea everything you have.

Chapter 9: Have a Purpose

Know your "Why"

Before doing anything, know your "why" for everything. Do not just do something because you see others doing it. Have a reason for what you are doing or want to do. Why do you want to leave your job? Why do you want to open a business? Why do you want to be your own boss? The stronger the answer to your "why," the more drive you will have throughout your journey. If you have a weak "why," you will have less of a drive and will find a way out instead of giving it everything you have.

If your "why" is something like "to support your family and provide for the loved ones around you," you will most likely push until you get what you want. You won't let anything get in your way because you have a purpose for your efforts and you want the outcome to become a reality. The mental standpoint you will have when you decide your "why" can be the deciding factor on how things will play out down the road. If your "why" is something basic and less of a priority, then you will not have the drive it takes to make it through the rough patches, and you'll leave it like it isn't a big deal.

Everything you do in life needs to have a purpose. Without purpose there is no direction for you to follow. Many people end up lost their entire lives because they have no answer to why they are living the life they are. Do not be that person! If you do not know already, figure out what your "why" is and what your purpose is in life. Stop waiting and watching time tick by. Do not have the misconception that you are going to change your life around when you get older, because I can promise you it will not play out the way you may be imagining it.

If you wait until you get older to change your life around, you may be setting yourself up to be trapped. You will live your life like a hamster running on the wheel, running but not really moving. If you are not living the life you want now, what makes you say you are going to make the change when there are more responsibilities in your life? There's always going to be things that come up, but if you do not go after what you want now, it will only make it tougher later on in life. For example, if you are single, have no kids or mortgage to pay, and you are still waiting for a better time to do what you want to instead of working for someone else, then you will never have the chance to leave your job later due to the responsibilities you will have with more on your plate. Take the risk now instead of holding off for a better time in life because there is no such thing as the "perfect time."

"Having a purpose is the difference between making a living and making a life."
-Tom Thiss-

Start making a life for yourself and not working for a living. Find something that makes you feel like you are not even doing work but you are having fun while you are making a life for yourself. Many people get into work for the capital it brings. For example, some people go to medical school just so they can get a six figure salary, but they can't stand to see blood. How does that make any sense? You have to be passionate about what you do in life or else you will live a very miserable life, no matter what your pay looks like. I've come across people who get paid $200k a year who are not happy with their lives. I've also come across people who run a food cart on the side of the road who are happier than ever. You have to love what you do before you go into something. Do not let money be the deciding factor for what you want to do in life.

If your life revolves around the money you make and you do not like what you do, you will find yourself in a worse situation than when you did not have anything. You may feel like your life was better before you had anything, and that's because you do not like what you do and money can never fix that. As corny as it sounds, you need to find your passion before you look for pay. Making a decision on what you want to do is what your life will revolve around, so choose wisely and know what you are getting into. Do your side of the research. Also, do as much homework as possible. Once you find something you like, check if it's in demand or not. Consider if it's in a saturated market or not. Once you find what works for you, dive in head-first. Do not waste a second because I can promise you there is someone else in the world working on something similar to what you are working on and who may be working twice as hard.

Go All In!

Give your venture or idea everything you have and I can promise you will see positive results. If you put in only half the effort, you will get only half the results. If you go "all in" and give it everything you have, you will get positive results. It's just about how much time and effort you put into something. When starting out, you may feel behind, but that's ok. Take everything one step at a time and really work on your craft. Do not think because someone else in your industry is ahead that you need to cut corners and catch up. You will gradually get there with hard work and the effort you put in. You will always feel behind when starting out and that's completely fine.

Learn to work on yourself and put all your efforts into the work you do. Do not think for a second that things will just be handed to you. You need to take action in order to see results in your life and build the life you see for yourself. There are too many people that want everything handed to them without working. Do not be that person. Instead throw all your chips into one basket and give everything you have to your idea or venture and I promise you will see results. I can't promise that you will be successful in the first thing you dive into, but the best part about all of it is that if you fail, you may actually learn and grow more than you would if you became a success right away.

The more you fail in life, the more you will learn. The more you learn, the more you will grow. I like to take my losses as lesson and learn everything I can from them. Not many people like to look at it that way, but some of the most successful people in the world will tell you that failure is one of the best gifts they were given. If it was not for their failure, they would have not grown and become the person they are now. You need to take your losses and turn them into lessons in order to grow and really get on the path toward success. Do not give up if things don't go your way, right away. Good things always take time and if you're someone who thinks you need to get lucky to be successful or that people who are successful are lucky, then you are lost. The people who are successful worked for it, and they deserve what they worked for. Are there people who have everything handed to them? Yes, but I do not look at that as a success. Success has to do with more than just money or materialism. Success has to do with the way you live your life day-to-day.

You can have all the money in the world but still feel poor. If you have no meaning to life, then you will always feel poor no matter how much money is in your bank account. The people in that bubble are not successful, and that lifestyle can lead to very tragic outcomes like drug overdoses or suicide. It has in the past. Success has to do with your mindset, your daily routine, how you approach life, and what you do. Have you ever heard that health is wealth? It's very true. You can ask any rich person who is ill if they would trade in all their money for their health back, 10 out of 10 times they will tell you; "Yes!"

In order to live a successful life and really enjoy what you do, you need to have purpose. Everyone has their own purpose. It could be working hard every day for loved ones, giving back, changing the world, etc. If you cannot find your purpose, you can live your entire life not having to worry about finances. But the other worries are the ones that are going to ruin your life inside and out because you see no true meaning to life. If you want to really find out for yourself, then the next time you are around someone who is "successful," really pay attention to the way they live and act. A successful person stays happy through their ups and downs. A successful person always tries to help the people around them. Everything is not just about money; they see life for what it actually is.

Successful people appreciate what they have and everything that happens to them. Many people have the wrong interpretation for success because of what they see on TV or on social media. What you don't see is the individual's actual life and how they live day and night. Watching them on a screen builds a misinterpretation of their life in your head. If you are someone who likes to dwell on the way others have it and the way others live, stop now! The things you are seeing are almost like virtual reality. Social media is mostly fake. The way most of the people on social media are living is completely different than the way they post and show themselves on the internet. They have the control to post whatever they want. Why would someone post something bad? Everything you see is positive most of the time. So it makes it look like the person's life is perfect when in reality it can be the complete opposite.

Trust the Process

Are you someone who doubts themselves? If you answered "yes," then you really need to take what you are about to read into account. Everyone has a voice in their head at one point or another that tells them they will not make it. It's a voice that tells you that "this is not for you" or "there is no way you are going to make it." Everyone goes through this, and the ones that make it out on top are the ones that trust the process and keep fighting.

Things are not going to magically happen overnight. It is going to take time and persistence. You need to be ready for the ride if you want to fight these voices and thoughts that you encounter. These are thoughts and voices that scare people away from reaching their potential limits in life. Everyone has a uniqueness to themselves on this planet, and only a few are able to realize and use it to their full potential. The fact that you read this whole book should tell you that you are willing to do what it takes to make the change in your life. It should push you to get what is meant for you. There is no roof to where you can be in life if you believe in yourself and everything you are trying to do.

You have to believe in what you are wanting to do before you even start. If you have any sort of negativity in your heart about what you are doing, you will only hold yourself back. Stay positive, believe in yourself no matter what others may think or say to you. The people that were crazy enough to think they could make a difference in the world are the ones that actually did! You need to believe in yourself like no one else will. Block all the noise from the outside and really tell yourself you can do it. Really believe it! The more you doubt yourself, the more opposition there will be against you. We have enough in the world against us already. Take the time now to stop being against yourself. You can be your own biggest enemy if you don't figure yourself out and go after what you want in life.

Go out and make things happen for yourself. No one is going to hold your hand and bring you to the steps of success. You need to build them on your own. It may take a while. When you do reach it and you start to see results in your life and your day-to-day living, you are going to love every moment of it. It will be well worth it when your life changes around and you look back at the time you took the jump. You need to take high risks to retain high rewards. Now is the time for you to do that. Stop waiting for the perfect moment and make the change you want to see. Everything is up to you and what you want to do with your life. So stop wasting time. I don't want you to have to read many books like this to make a vast change in your life. Let this be the last book you read like this. There is no reason you should have to read books like this and listen to videos that get you motivated because then you are not truly motivating yourself and pushing yourself but you are depending on some else to push you.

You need to love the process and push yourself every day. You need to be the one that drives yourself. If you rely on others to push you and drive you, it can hold you back from achieving what you want and where you want to be. Watching motivational videos and listening to motivational lectures can be good at times, but to use them to motivate you every day is giving you fake motivation. You are relying on your motivation to come from someone else. It is most effective if it comes from you. If you are someone who loves watching motivational videos, ask yourself, are they really driving you or helping you? Or are you binge watching more without putting forth the work that's supposed to come from watching these videos?

It almost becomes like TV, when you continue to watch these videos it may make you feel great at the moment, but it really is not giving you organic motivation. Organic motivation comes from your daily grind and the effort you are putting in. That is what will bring you true motivation and push you to do more with your life, compared to what someone is saying behind a screen. I'm not taking anything away from influencers because they help change lives every day. But know your limits and know what it's going to take to push yourself past your limits.

Conclusion

This book was written for people to reach their true potential. If you are someone who is being pushed around in life and are not where you want to be or working toward where you want to be, then you need to really evaluate your life up to this point and ask yourself, what can I do to truly change my life around for the better? We covered many topics in this book. This book may not be the best book written on self-improvement, but you have the opportunity in your hand to really make the change you would like to see. Know that you do not have to do something you hate every day for a paycheck.

You now have the opportunity to do something different and make an impact with the way the world is moving today. If you haven't noticed for yourself already, this book should have helped you open your eyes to reality and the opportunities that are in the world for the taking. It is up to you and me to make the change and pass it on. We were all put on this earth for a reason. To live life wasting time is selfish. You have the opportunity many people in the world don't, and if you are wasting it, how does that make you worthy of being in the good situation you are in?

I hope everyone who reads this book at least learns one thing from it and implements it in their daily life. If you read everything, then I hope it motivates you to do more and that it pushes you toward greatness. Take the time now and think of someone this book can help benefit, and please pass it on! I encourage you to push as many people as you can and help as many people as you can because the world lies in our hands. It's what we do with our opportunities today that will determine the results tomorrow. If we help destroy the world then there will be nothing left of it tomorrow, but if we help build it only God knows where we can take it in the future.

Once you do have something good going for you please always remember to give back, whether it's to the community or people suffering around the globe. We will not be on this planet forever. There will come a time when you get old and there will not be much left for you to do. You may not even be able to physically get anything accomplished due to old age. Take advantage of the abilities you have now and really strive to make something happen in the world that will make a difference. All the materialistic belongings will vanish and the only thing that will remain are your good deeds. Push yourself every day and know that you only have limited time; so stop wasting it and go make something happen without making excuses. Go out and MAKE THE CHANGE.